MODERN
SPOKEN ITALIAN:

PART A

Italian Language Materials
Available from AUDIO-FORUM

Courses

Modern Spoken Italian, Part A. 8 cassettes and 124-page book.

Modern Spoken Italian, Part B. 8 cassettes and 136-page book.

Other Italian Language Materials

Il Nuovo Testamento. Riveduta version, recorded by Milazzo. 16 cassettes.

Italian Culture Capsules [Recorded in English]. Insights into Italian customs and language usage. 1 cassette.

96 Broad Street, Guilford, CT 06437 ● (203) 453-9794

MODERN SPOKEN ITALIAN:

Active Italian Communication

PART A

by
Elaine Vertucci Baran

A Division of Jeffrey Norton Publishers, Inc.
Guilford, CT   London, England

MODERN SPOKEN ITALIAN: ACTIVE ITALIAN COMMUNICATION PART A

ISBN: 1-57970-075-6

Published by Audio-Forum, a division of Jeffrey Norton Publishers, Inc.
96 Broad Street, Guilford, CT 06437

PREFACE

Modern Spoken Italian is the final product of a curriculum development project begun at Brookdale Community College, Lincroft, New Jersey in the summer of 1978. The author, unable to find suitable (i.e. modern and natural) materials that truly stressed communicative competence in Italian, decided to develop her own Level I course in order to meet the needs of the community college students in her area.

One of these needs was a desire to pursue an independent approach to learning a language. Therefore, in order to maximize the students' chances for success, both in the classroom and in an independent manner, the typical text-book formula was abandoned.

In its place, a complete text study-guide was developed along with cassette tapes. The cassette tapes were developed not merely as an accompaniment, but as an absolute, integral part of the course, that completes the whole. Testing, too, was incorporated into the taped program as an extension of each unit, so that it became a true learning tool that makes use of several kinds of recorded exercises.

The course was then implemented as part of the regular course schedule and later as a radio course with the tapes broadcast on the college's own radio station for students who wanted a truly independent approach to learning Italian.

It has met with much success in the past two and one-half years as an independent study course. Several elements have now been refined to help insure that the totally independent learner can equalize the communicative success of the Brookdale students. It is the author's firm belief that this can be achieved by carefully following the strategy of the program as explained in the "Notes to the Learner" which follows this preface.

The author wishes to acknowledge some of the many people who helped make Modern Spoken Italian a reality. She gratefully thanks all those students who patiently awaited new units and who made excellent suggestions, many of which have been incorporated into the final product.

A sincere thank you is extended to Tina Vertucci, Nicoletta Squillante, Antonio Blaser, Lilliana Francavilla

V

and Luisa Francavilla who provided the tape voices and to Bart Coma who produced the taped materials. The author notes especially Dan Baran for all of the drawings, Susan Corsetti London for developing the taped culture capsules, Prof. Albert Eyde of Brookdale, whose original format in Spanish inspired the present Modern Spoken Italian and Deborah Gardner whose excellent typing produced the final manuscript.

Special thanks are extended to Beatriz Zeller, Bart Coma, Nicoletta Squillante and Lilliana Francavilla by the author, for countless other tasks performed on her behalf.

The author appreciates the efforts of the administration of Brookdale Community College, in particular Dr. Rita Donahue, Dean of the Applied Humanities Institute, in facilitating publication of these materials. She is indebted to the Instructional Development Laboratory of Brookdale whose facilities were used to produce the taped materials. She gratefully acknowledges Jeffrey Norton publishers for its original interest in publishing the Italian materials and for much patience and cooperation in awaiting the completed project.

Finally, she thanks her family, her husband Carl and her children, Cara and Jonathan. Their cooperation and loving support truly helped Modern Spoken Italian come into being.

Elaine Vertucci Baran
April, 1981

NOTES TO THE LEARNER

Modern Spoken Italian is composed of ten units of written instruction complemented by ten units of taped instruction. These units are preceded by an introductory pronunciation lesson that is also both written and taped.

The written units are divided into the following sections - Basic Sentences, Dialogs or Narratives, Questions, Supplements, Grammatical Explanations, Drills (repetition, substitution, cued question and answer, question and answer), Review Questions and Learning Activities. The taped units correspond exactly to the written units up to and including all drills. The Review Questions and the Learning Activities are not recorded.

At the end of each taped unit you will find an informative Culture Capsule on the many different aspects of Italian life and language. Also, your mastery of each unit is evaluated in a three part "Test Yourself" section at the end of each taped unit. These two sections are not in the text, with the exception of the pictures of Part II of the "Test Yourself".

You will also find some lively drawings interspersed throughout the text and you are encouraged to use them as conversation starters about the units you have covered.

For you, the Learner, to achieve maximum benefit from these materials, you are urged to use the written and taped materials to complement each other by following this suggested pattern:

FIRST: Go carefully through the Introductory Unit and do all of the repetitions and short exercises. Good pronunciation and stress are very important and this unit will enable you to become familiar with the sounds and symbols of the Italian language and thereby give you a comfortable entry into Unit I.

SECOND: In Unit I and in all succeeding units start by listening carefully and then repeating the Basic Sentences. Try not to use the written materials the very first time you listen and repeat. See how much you can do without the written words. Try this technique for both the Basic Sentences and the Dialogs/Narratives. Then practice saying them until you feel comfortable with them and understand their meanings. They are your first introduction to the vocabulary and grammatical patterns of each unit.

THIRD: Go on to the Dialog or Narrative which is a recombination of the vocabulary and structures of the Basic Sentences. In all cases it is written in a very conversational style that prompts questions. Practice the Dialog/Narrative until you feel confident to answer questions on it.

FOURTH: Procede to the questions. Both questions and answers are on tape for every unit. However, after Unit 6, the written answers are not provided. This is done at this point to encourage you to supply your own answer based on the dialog and then reinforce it with the tape. Throughout the units, try not to rely too heavily on the tape or the written word to provide you with the correct answer. Cover up the answers, provide your ówn, then uncover them and listen to the tape response.

FIFTH: Continue on to the Supplement and practice it in the same fashion as the Basic Sentences and the Dialogs.

SIXTH: At this point grammatical explanations begin. We have tried to make them as straightforward and uncomplicated as possible. All grammatical points are followed by several types of drills that go from a very simple repetition to questions and answers that involve several grammatical operations. With the exception of the repetitions and some of the question and answer drills, all other drills are not answered in the text. The tape provides the correct response. Space is provided in the text for you to answer them. This is a fine way of learning the points presented. Listen to the drill, answer it orally and in writing; go back and check your answer. You may choose to do all drills orally or all drills in writing first. You have a great deal of flexibility here. Although the author prefers listening and speaking first, some learners find that writing first enables them to better understand the spoken word. Therefore, take the text and the tape and find which method works best for you. Be very sure to allow yourself enough time to cover all of the drills presented thoroughly before you go on to the Review Questions.

SEVENTH: You have now arrived at a point in the unit which expects a good grasp of the materials presented;

the Review Questions, Learning Activities and finally the taped "Test Yourself Section". The Review Questions are not recorded and many encourage original responses not based on the text. The author suggests that you do these both orally and in writing even if speaking is your main concern. You should be quite successful in this – especially if you have <u>looked</u> and <u>listened</u> carefully as you worked through the unit.

The Learning Activities are provided to give you some more practice in the language. Many of them were originally designed for a group situation, but the author encourages you to try them and urges you to look for someone to speak to and work with if possible in Italian. Get out and practice your Italian if at all possible from the very beginning of the text.

EIGHTH: Finally, the "Test Yourself" section completes each unit. This is not only an excellent exercise to determine your mastery of the materials, it is also another opportunity to extend your abilities in Italian. It is divided into three parts: a Dictation in which you take a dictation in Italian and then answer the dictation questions in Italian; a Listening Comprehension exercise in which you listen to the tape and then select an answer from a page of drawings in your text; and a Listen and Write exercise which evaluates your ability to remember what has been said in Italian and then write about it.

After you have completed the "Test Yourself" section, do not hesitate to read aloud your responses to Parts I and II and record your voice if you wish. Also, the drawings of Part II make for an excellent conversation stimulus and review of materials; especially if you are working with another person. Use the other drawings and map of Italy for conversation starters or to summarize some of the material from the units.

As stated in the Preface, the author firmly believes that by following the steps outlined here you will achieve a maximum amount of communicative competence in this first level of Italian. You are now ready to begin. Start by listening to the Introductory Unit.

CONTENTS

XI

INTRODUCTORY UNIT - EXERCISES

Exercise 1. The Italian Alphabet

		Foreign Letters:
a - a	m - emme	
b - bi	n - enne	
c - ci	o - o	j - i lunga
d - di	p - pi	k - cappa
e - e	q - cu	x - ics
f - effe	r - erre	y - ipsilon
g - gi	s - esse	w - vu doppio
h - acca	t - ti	
i - i	u - u	
l - elle	v - vu	
	z - zeta	

Exercise 2. Accents

Acute - perché, sé, né   Grave - è, ritornerò,
                                    città, sì, già, più

Exercise 3.
e (and) è (is)   da (from) dà (gives)
si (himself) sì (yes)   by
     herself   la (the) là(there)
se (if) sè (oneself)

Exercise 4.
Dov'è, l'amico, d'America, un'università, c'è

Exercise 5. Stress
A. Second to last:
corso
amico   finestra   studentessa   albergo
basta   Alberto   bello   studente
         Caterina   pesche
B. Third to Last:
automobile fabbrica   isola
nobile   lettera   simpatico
telefono   abito

C. Last Syllable:

città   così
università   trentatrè
difficoltà   però
             perché

D. Fourth from last:
abitano
desiderano
recuperano

Exercise 6.

1. pri mo
2. cu gi no
3. au to mo bi le
4. cit ta
5. per che
6. bel lo
7. al ber go
8. i so la
9. a bi ta no
10. Ro ber to
11. fi ne stra
12. co si
13. u ti le
14. og gi
15. ot ti mo
16. stu den te
17. dif fi col ta
18. a des so
19. dif fi ci le
20. ve de re
21. mez zo
22. u ni ver si ta
23. A me ri ca
24. do ve
25. an no

Exercise 7. Part A

/a/	/e/	/i/	/o/
casa	arriverderci	signorina	oliva
Anna	bene	libri	cosa
classe	egli	Gina	vestito
adesso	eccellente	dico	dove
amore	sete	bambini	sono

/u/
luna
uno
studia
tu
utile

1. Questa lezione è difficile.
2. Gina, i libri sono eccellenti!
3. Dove sono i bambini?
4. Adesso, Anna ha sete.
5. Amore, dov'è il vestito?

Part B. 1.   2.   3.   4.   5.   6.   7.
         8.   9.   10.

Exercise 8.
lei, grazie, fiore, studia, olio, miei, vuoi, suoi, tuoi.

1. Vorrei cambiare i miei assegni.   3. Grazie, Maria.
2. Dove sono i tuoi vestiti?   Buon giorno Gianni.

Exercise 9.
duo	liceo	lucciola	scimmia
autostrada	scuola	ciao	eroe
aiuola	fagioli	mille	aula
vigilia	cuoca	geografia	

Exercise 10. Consonants b, f, m, n, v.
basta	freddo	mattina	no	diverso
sbaglio	affatto	calma	noi	vestito
abitare	cifra	permesso	alunno	vita
cabina	fabbrica	mezzo	penna	diavolo
	differente	anima	gennaio	chiave

"C" Sounds: casa cuoco ciao   anche
            cena c'è   chiama poco
            chi   camicia faccia liceo
            che   cibo   chiuso

"D" Sounds: dad   - dare   ended - andare
            dear   - dove   paid - undici
            indeed - indiano

"G" Sounds:
   Hard - vago, lago, laghi, albergo, alberghi
   Soft - giorno, Gina, gente, gennaio, giovedì, oggi
          passeggiata

"gli" and "gn" Sounds: gli, degli, luglio, biglietto,
                       meglio, voglio, gnocchi, gnomo,
                       lavagna, cognome, cagnolino,
                       bisogno.

"H" (no sound): ho, ha, hanno.

"L" Sounds: lazy - loro, long - lungo, always - allora
            gladly - volo, light - luce.

"P" Sounds: posso, pane, papà, aperitivo, capo, perché,
            capisco, passeggiata, appunto.

"Q" Sounds: qui, questo, quale, Pasqua, quindi

"R" Sounds: single - Roma, Franco, prego, rumore, ragazza
            double - burro, arriverderci, carrozza,
                     marrone, arrivo

"S" Sounds: unvoiced - signorina, benissimo, pasta, storia,
            succede. voiced - casa, cosa, rosa, frase,
            così. sc and sch - ascolto, dischi, scusi,
            scappare, pesche. sc and e or i - sciare,
            uscire, pesce, conoscere, finisce

"T" Sounds: time - tempo, return - tornare, television-
            televisione, doctor - dottore, art - arte.
"Z" Sounds: <u>unvoiced</u> - zio, zuppa, pazienza, piazza,
            forza: <u>voiced</u> - zero, mezzo, zanzara, pranzo,
            azzurro.
Pairs: zio - zero, zuppa - mezzo, pizza - zanzara,
       piazza - pranzo, forza - azzurro.

1. voiced, unvoiced   6. voiced, unvoiced
2. voiced, unvoiced   7. voiced, unvoiced
3. voiced, unvoiced   8. voiced, unvoiced
4. voiced, unvoiced   9. voiced, unvoiced
5. voiced, unvoiced   10. voiced, unvoiced

<u>Double consonants - single - double pairs</u>:
camino - cammino   fato - fatto
capello - cappello   pena - penna
sete   - sette   copia - coppia
sono   - sonno   rosa - rossa
casa   - cassa   pala - palla
caro   - carro
<u>Double consonant words</u>: pizza, quattro, babbo, panna,
mezzo, arrivo, allora, buffo, mamma.
1. single, double   6. single, double
2. single, double   7. single, double
3. single, double   8. single, double
4. single, double   9. single, double
5. single, double   10. single, double

<u>Sentences</u>:
1. I giovani vanno alla cassa.
2. Dove sono i miei libri?
3. Arrivo a Roma domani?
4. Che cosa cerchi, Maria?
5. Ciao Roberto, come stai oggi?
6. Ci sono molti turisti qui.
7. Gli studenti vanno a lezione.
8. Sono le quattro e mezza.
9. Mi piace sciare a Cortina.
10. La professoressa ha molta pazienza con gli alunni.

OVERVIEW OF UNIT I

This is an introduction to Modern Spoken Italian. We will learn quite a few simple greetings and names and expressions that take in some of the sounds of the Italian language. You will also be introduced to several forms of the two verbs to be, the verb to go and the verb to call or to be named.

GRAMMAR POINTS PRESENTED

1. Asking questions in Italian.
2. Yes and No answers.
3. Numbers 1 - 12
4. Time on the hour.
5. Several present tense forms of the verbs to be, to go and to call (including the informal "you" form).

SECTION I BASIC SENTENCES

Practice repeating the following sentences after the speaker on the tape. Learn the Italian sentences and their English meanings well.

CIAO!	HI!
È una ragazza.	(She) is a girl.
Si chiama Carla.	Her name is Carla. (literally: she calls herself Carla)
È un ragazzo.	(He) is a boy.
Si chiama Paolo.	His name is Paolo. (literally: he calls himself Paul)
Carla sta bene.	Carla is fine.
Anche Paolo sta bene.	Paul is fine too.

NOTES: È (is) is a form of the verb "to be" in Italian. There are 2 verbs "to be" in Italian. Sta is a form of the other verb "to be".

ch in Italian is pronounced like the hard 'c' in the English word call.

1

NOTE: The letters che are pronounced much like the letter
      'k' in English, but in a short crisp manner.

SECTION II DIALOG
      Practice the following dialog in Italian with the
speakers on the tape. Learn the entire Italian conversation and the English meanings.

CIAO!   HI!

Paolo: Ciao, Carla, come   Hi Carla, how are you?
       stai?
Carla: Bene, grazie. E tu?   Fine thanks. And you?
Paolo: Benino. Dove vai?   O.K.(or fine) Where are you
                                  going?
Carla: Al cinema.   To the movies.

NOTES: Ci (as in cinema and ciao) is a soft sound in
       Italian much like the ch of 'church' in English.

SECTION III QUESTIONS
1. Come si chiama la   Si chiama Carla.
   ragazza?
2. Come sta la ragazza?   Sta bene.
3. Come si chiama il   Si chiama Paolo.
   ragazzo?
4. Sta bene il ragazzo?   Sì, sta bene.
5. Dove va Carla?   Al cinema.

NOTES: Come as a question word may mean what or how.
       Sì (yes) is written with an accent over the i
       to distinguish it from the same word with other
       meanings.

SECTION IV SUPPLEMENT
      Learn the Italian phrases of this section and their
meanings in English. Practice saying the expressions
after the speaker on the tape.

A. GREETINGS AND GOODBYES

Buon giorno   Hello, good day
Buona sera   Hello, good evening (from
                                  late afternoon to late night)

2

Buona notte	Goodnight (in the sense of leave taking)
Buona notte signore	Goodnight sir
Buona notte signora	Goodnight madam
Buona notte signorina	Goodnight miss

NOTE: The titles signore, signora, signorina are used very commonly with or without last names in Italy.

Arriverderla	Goodbye (formal)
Arriverderci	Goodbye (informal)
Ciao	Hi (hello) and Goodbye (friendly and informal)
Ci vediamo	See you (literally: we'll see each other, usually meaning soon).
A più tardi	See you later (until later)
A domani	Until tomorrow

B. ASKING NAMES

Come si chiama? (formal)	What's your name?
Come ti chiami? (informal)	What's your name?
Mi chiamo Gianni Fanelli.	My name is Johnny Fanelli.
Mi chiamo Elena.	My name is Ellen.

NOTE: The informal 'you' form of verbs is used to address relatives, close friends, children or students up to about age 17. In almost all other instances, the formal 'you' form is used. In the typical Italian university situation, students use the informal form with each other and the formal form with the instructor.

C. HOW ARE YOU AND RESPONSES

Come sta? (formal)	How are you?
Come stai? (informal)	How are you?
Bene.	Fine.
Non c'è male.	Not bad. (fine)
Benino.	O.K. (fine)
Abbastanza bene.	Pretty well.
Bennissimo.	Very well

C. (continued)

Male.   Bad, not well.

SECTION V YES AND NO IN ITALIAN and QUESTIONS

    SÌ means YES
    NO means NO

Examples:
Carla è una ragazza?   Sì, Carla e una ragazza.
Is Carla a girl?   Yes, Carla is a girl.

Paolo è una ragazza?   No, Paolo è un ragazzo.
Is Paul a girl?   No, Paul is a boy.

Practice answering the following questions in Italian.
Answer the questions according to the cues in parenthesis.

Examples:
Carla sta bene? (yes)   Sì, Carla sta bene.
Anche Gianni sta bene?(no)   No, Gianni sta male.
La ragazza si chiama
 Carla? (no, Gina)   No, si chiama Gina.
Sta bene Mario? (yes)   Sì, Mario sta benissimo.

CUED QUESTION - ANSWER DRILL

1. È una ragazza? (Sì)
2. È Carla? (Sì)
3. Gianni sta benne? (No, male)
4. La ragazza si chiama Carla? (No, Gina)
5. Sta bene Mário? (Sì, benissimo)

NOTES: As you can see from the previous drill, asking
questions is not difficult in Italian. You don't have
to change the sentence word order; your voice <u>intonation</u>
makes it a question in speaking and the <u>question mark</u>
makes it a question in writing. However, you may change
the word order if you want (as in question #5 in the
previous drill) and place the subject at the end of the
sentence or right after the verb (Sta Maria bene?): but
most Italians like the simplest way of making a question.

4

SECTION VI NUMBERS AND TIME EXPRESSIONS ON THE HOUR

Learn the Italian numbers of this section and their meanings in English. Practice saying them after the speaker on the tape.

A. REPETITION DRILL

0	zero	7	sette
1	uno (una)	8	otto
2	due	9	nove
3	tre	10	dieci
4	quattro	11	undici
5	cinque	12	dodici
6	sei		

NOTE: Stress is on the underlined syllable.

B. REPETITION DRILL - Practice the following time expressions on the hour in Italian. Learn their meanings in English. Practice saying them after the speaker on the tape.

Che ora è?	What time is it?
È mezzogiorno.	It's noon.
È mezzanotte.	It's midnight.
È l'una.	It's one o'clock.
Sono le due.	It's two o'clock.
Sono le tre.	It's three o'clock.
Sono le quattro.	It's four o'clock.
Sono le cinque.	It's five o'clock.
Sono le sei.	It's six o'clock.
Sono le sette.	It's seven o'clock.
Sono le otto.	It's eight o'clock.
Sono le nove.	It's nine o'clock.
Sono le dieci.	It's ten o'clock.
Sono le undici.	It's eleven o'clock.
Sono le dodici precise.	It's twelve on the dot.

NOTE: Notice that una is used for one o'clock instead of the number one (uno). Also, a singular verb form is used (è) for one o'clock, noon and midnight. It is important that this form always be accented to distinguish it from e meaning 'and'.

Sono is the plural form of the verb and is used for all the forms except those already mentioned.

5

C. Respond to the question - CHE ORA È? - in the following exercise: (NOT RECORDED)

1. 8:00	5. 1:00
2. 12 midnight	6. 12 noon
3. 7:00 on the dot	7. 11:00
4. 3:00	

SECTION VII   REVIEW QUESTIONS (NOT RECORDED)

Respond freely to the following questions using complete sentences whenever possible. If a cue appears after the question, use it when answering.

1. Come stai?	6. Dove vai?
2. Buon giorno.	7. Come si chiama il ragazzo?
3. È una ragazza? (Si)	8. È mezzogiorno? (No,
4. Sta bene Mario? (No)	midnight)
5. Che ora è?	9. Come ti chiami?
	10. Dove va Carla?

SECTION VIII   LEARNING ACTIVITIES

1. Write an original conversation between two people, in the informal form, using the expressions and verbs you have learned in this unit. Practice your conversation aloud.

2. By answering the following questions write a short paragraph about Carla. Omit the words 'yes' or 'no' as part of the answer in the paragraph sentences.
a. È una ragazza?   d. Dove va?
b. Come si chiama?   e. Che ora è?
c. Come sta la ragazza?

3. Answer this question: CHE ORA È? Provide the most logical choice based on the cues given.
a. Time to eat lunch_____.
b. The beginning of the new year._____.
c. Thirteen hours in Military time._____.

6

UNIT II

OVERVIEW OF UNIT II

In this unit we will continue to introduce verb forms and do all of the verb 'to go'. We will practice the subject pronoun forms for all verbs in Italian. We will continue numbers and time, make negative statements and express likes and dislikes.

GRAMMAR POINTS PRESENTED

1. The expression 'ecco'.
2. Singular and plural subject pronouns.
3. Present tense of verb 'andare' (to go).
4. Negatives.
5. The numbers 13 - 60.
6. Time expressions on the minute.

SECTION I BASIC SENTENCES
Practice saying the following sentences after the speaker on the tape. Learn the Italian sentences and their English meanings.

ANDIAMO A LEZIONE!	LET'S GO TO CLASS!
Carla va a lezione.	Carla is going to class.
Lei va con Silvia.	She is going with Silvia.
Ecco Gianni.	There's Gianni.
È tardi.	It's late.
Vanno assieme.(insieme)	They are going together.

NOTE: Both assieme and insieme mean together.
Ecco (here is, here are, there is, there are) is a very useful little word since it has both singular and plural meanings. It is used when pointing to or pointing out objects or people.

SECTION II DIALOG

Carla: Ecco Gianni.	There's Gianni.
Silvia: Anche lui va a lezione.	He's going to class too.

8

DIALOG (continued)

Carla: Ciao Gianni, tu vai   Hi Gianni, are you going
     a lezione?   to class?
Gianni: Sì, ci vado adesso.   Yes, I'm going there now.
Carla: Sali, (noi) andiamo   Get in. We'll go together.
     assieme.
Gianni: Tante grazie, è   Thanks a lot, it's late.
     tardi.

NOTE: Although the subject pronouns are not needed here
they are used so you may familiarize yourself with them
and the verb forms that they take.

SECTION III QUESTIONS

1. Dove va Carla?   Carla va a lezione.
2. Anche Silvia va?   Sì, anche Silvia va.
3. Chi c'è?   C'è Gianni.
4. Dove va Gianni?   Gianni va a lezione.
5. Vanno assieme?   Sì, vanno assieme.

NOTE: In question #3, instead of ecco, c'è is used to
indicate that Gianni is located in a place; that he
'is there'. We will learn more about c'è (there is)
later. C'è states that someone is there; it doesn't point
out.

SECTION IV SUPPLEMENT

A. THANK YOU'S and YOU'RE WELCOMES

    Grazie   Thank you
    Grazie tanto   Thanks a lot
    Tante grazie   " " "
    Prego   You're welcome
    Di niente   (It's) nothing
    Non c'è di che   Don't mention it

B. EXPRESSING LIKES and DISLIKES

    Ti piace?   Do you like it?
    (Ti is the informal   (lit: Is it pleasing
     form)   to you?)
    Le piace?   Do you like it?
    (Le is the formal form)
    Ti piace il ristorante? Do you like the
                      restaurant?
    Le piace la lezione? Do you like the class?

9

LIKES and DISLIKES (continued)

Sì, mi piace.	Yes, I like it. (lit: It is pleasing to me)
No, non mi piace.	No, I don't like it.
Mi piace molto.	I like it a lot.
Mi piace moltissimo.	I really like it.
Mi piace abbastanza.	I like it quite a bit.
Non mi piace affatto!	I don't like it at all!

SECTION V SUBJECT PRONOUNS
    You have already been introduced to most of the
subject pronouns in Italian. One set of subject pronouns
(as in English) is used for all verbs.

A. REPETITION - Singular Subject Pronouns - Learn the
following singular subject pronouns and their English
meanings.

io = I	lui = He
tu = You (informal)	lei = She
Lei = You (formal)	

NOTE: There are two YOU singular forms in Italian.
      Tu and Lei.
      The 'informal you' or tu as we mentioned in the
      first lesson is used when talking to good friends,
      family members, relatives or children. Lei is the
      'formal you' and is used in more formal situations
      or to show respect for another person.
      Lei is usually capitalized when it means 'you' and
      not capitalized when it means 'she'. In conversa-
      tion,i.e. spoken Italian, the context should
      logically tell you which one is being used.

B. REPETITION - Plural Subject Pronouns - Learn the
following plural subject pronouns and their English
meanings.

      noi = We   voi = You (informal) loro = They,you
                                              (formal)

NOTE: Although you has 2 plural forms, it has become
      very common in Italy to use the voi form almost
      exclusively and thereby reserve the loro form only
      for the most formal of situations. Therefore,
      throughout our text you will voi used exclusively

Plural Subject Pronouns (continued)

in place of the <u>loro</u> form.

SECTION VI <u>VERB</u> - <u>ANDARE</u> (To go)
In Italian 101 we are learning verbs only in the present tense - the here and now. You have already been introduced to most of the forms of the verb <u>andare</u> - <u>to go</u> in the present tense. Every verb in Italian is defined by a form which corresponds to the English 'to' form, as in 'to listen', 'to speak' and 'to go'. In Italian this form is one word and always ends in the letters <u>re</u>. It is called the infinitive.

A.   Example: <u>anda</u> - <u>re</u> meaning 'to go'.

Study the following singular forms of the verb <u>andare</u>:

Io vado adesso.	I'm going now.
Tu vai adesso.	You're going now.
Lei va adesso.	You (formal) are going now.
Lui va adesso.	He is going now.
Lei va adesso.	She is going now.

NOTE: The present can also be translated into English as 'I go' and 'I do go'.

B. REPETITION DRILL - Practice the following with the tape, learning meanings and Italian forms:

Io vado adesso	I'm going now.
Tu vai adesso.	You're going now.
Lei va adesso.	You're going now.
Mario va adesso.	Mario is going now.
Lui va adesso.	He's going now.
Carla va adesso.	Carla is going now.
Lei va adesso.	She is going now.

C. SUBSTITUTION DRILL - In the following exercises you will be asked to repeat a sentence, listen to, or see a cue: then repeat the sentence and substitute the cue into an appropriate position in the original sentence.

11

SUBSTITUTION DRILL (continued)

Example: Io vado a lezione.

    Tu_____   Lei (formale)_____

NOTE: Whenever the formal you is wanted, you will hear
      Lei (formale).

TAPE:	Io vado a lezione.
STUDENT:	Io vado a lezione.
CUE:	Tu
STUDENT:	Tu vai a lezione.
TAPE:	Tu vai a lezione.
CUE:	Lei (formale)
STUDENT:	Lei va a lezione.
TAPE:	Lei va a lezione.

The tape will always reinforce and provide the correct
substitution.

D. SUBSTITUTION DRILL

Io vado al cinema.   Lei (formale)_____

Lei_____   Io_____

Tu_____   Mario_____

E. SUBSTITUTION DRILL

Silvia va adesso.   Io_____

Tu_____   Lei (formale)_____

Lui_____   Lei_____

SECTION VII   PLURAL FORMS

A.Study the following plural forms of the verb ANDARE.

Noi andiamo adesso.   We're going now.

Voi andate adesso.   You're going now.

Loro vanno adesso.   They're going now.

B. Practice the following with the tape, learning
   meanings and Italian forms.

Noi andiamo assieme.   We're going together.

12

Plural Forms - Andare (continued)

Gianni ed io andiamo assieme.	Gianni and I are going together.
Voi andate assieme.	You are going together.
Mario e Gianni vanno assieme.	Mario and Gianni are going together.
Silvia e Carla vanno assieme.	Silvia and Carla are going together.
Loro vanno assieme.	They're going together.

NOTE: 'E' (and) followed by a vowel is normally written
      ed and pronounced much like the name ED in English.

      Whenever io is part of a plural subject, the form
      is always the 'we' form of the verb.

C. SUBSTITUTION DRILL (Go back to Section VI-C if you
still have problems doing a substitution drill)

Noi andiamo al cinema.	Voi_____
Loro_____	Carla ed io_____
Gianni e Silvia_____	

SECTION VIII NEGATIVES
     A sentence is made negative in Italian by placing
non in front of the verb. Non actually means not in
Italian.
Example:

Lui non va al cinema.	He's not going to the movies.
Voi non andate adesso.	You're not going now.
Mario non va a lezione.	Mario isn't going to class.

A. REPETITION DRILL
     Gianni non va a lezione.
     Io non vado adesso.
     Voi non andate assieme.
     Loro non vanno al cinema.
     Tu non vai al cinema.
     Lei non va adesso.
     Carla non va al cinema.
     Lei (formale) non va a lezione.

B. SUBSTITUTION DRILL

Io non vado al ristorante.   Silvia _____
Tu_____   Voi_____
Loro_____

C. TRANSFORMATION DRILL - Repeat the following sentences
changing them to the negative form.

Example: CUE: Carla va a lezione.
         STUDENT: Carla non va a lezione.
         TAPE: Carla non va a lezione.

1. Io vado al cinema._____
2. Silvia va a lezione._____
3. Noi andiamo adesso._____
4. Gianni e Carla vanno assieme._____
5. Lei va al ristorante._____

SECTION IX NUMBERS 13-60

13 tredici	29 ventinove
14 quattordici	30 trenta
15 quindici	31 trentuno
16 sedici	32 trentadue
17 diciasette	33 trentatrè
18 diciotto	38 trentotto
19 diciannove	40 quaranta
20 venti	41 quarantuno
21 ventuno	44 quarantaquattro
22 ventidue	48 quarantotto
23 ventitrè	50 cinquanta
24 ventiquattro	51 cinquantuno
25 venticinque	55 cinquantacinque
26 ventisei	58 cinquantotto
27 ventisette	60 sessanta
28 ventotto	

NOTE: Underlined portion indicates stress for pronunciation
     Venti, trenta, quaranta, cinquanta all drop their
final vowel before combining with uno or otto. Ventitrè,
trentatrè, etc. require the accent on the final e.

14

SECTION X TIME EXPRESSIONS ON THE MINUTE

e - as you know, means and
mezzo (or mezza) means half.
un quarto means quarter (as in quarter of an hour)
meno means minus (as in before the hour)

NOTE: Italians sometimes use 24 hour time, particularly
for train schedules and the hours of scheduled events.
You may want to use it to avoid confusion as to day or
evening.

A. REPETITION

1:30	È l'una e mezza.
2:30	Sono le due e mezzo.
6:30	Sono le sei e mezzo.
1:15	È l'una e un quarto.
4:15	Sono le quattro e un quarto.
1:45	Sono le due meno un quarto or
	È l'una e quarantacinque.
9:45	Sono le nove e quarantacinque or
	Sono le dieci meno un quarto.
11:02	Sono le undici e due.
11:23	Sono le undici e ventitrè.
12:30	È mezzogiorno e mezzo (Noon)
12:30	È mezzanotte e mezza. (Midnight)

B. Respond to the question - CHE ORA È? - in the
following exercise. (Not recorded)

1. 8:45   6. 11:45
2. 3:45   7. 12:15 (midnight)
3. 9:38   8. 1:30
4.10:15   9. 3:23
5.12:30 (noon)

SECTION XI REVIEW QUESTIONS (Not recorded)
Respond freely to the following questions using
complete sentences whenever possible. If a cue appears
after the question, use it when answering.

1.Gianni va a lezione?   2. Che ora è?

15

REVIEW QUESTIONS (continued)
3. Translate into Italian: There's Mario.
4. Ti piace il ristorante?
5. Carla e Silvia vanno al cinema?
6. Sono le tre? (No - 4:15)
7. Dove va Mario?
8. Le piace la lezione? (No)
9. Grazie.......
10.Chi va al cinema?
11.Translate into Italian - You(formal)are going to class?

SECTION XII LEARNING ACTIVITIES
1. Fill in the blank spaces with any logical word.
a. Silvia va a _____ .   d. È_____.
b. Ecco_____.   e. Gianni e Silvia___assieme.
c. _____ lui va.
2. From among the list A choices, express your likes and
dislikes using as many expressions from list B as you can.
A.   B.
il cinema   Sì, mi piace.
hockey   No, non mi piace.
ice-cream   Mi piace molto.
disco   Mi piace moltissimo.
T.V.   Mi piace abbastanza.
Andare a lezione.   Non mi piace affatto.
3. Fill in the spaces with the proper form of the verb
ANDARE.
a. Silvia dove_____?   d. E Maria e Carla? Oh!
b. Io___al cinema con Gianni. Anche loro_____.
c. Voi___adesso? Sì.
4. Add or subtract the following in Italian.
a.tredici+quaranta=___   d.quarantaquattro-tredici=___
b.cinquantuno+tre=___   e.diciannove-due=___
c.ventuno-otto=___   f.ventisette+trentatrè=___
5.Compose an original story of about 5 lines about yourself. Use forms of the verb andare in the affirmative
and the negative. Also use some or all of the following
vocabulary and expressions in your short story. Read it
aloud.
ristorante   è mezzogiorno
mi piace   mezzanotte
adesso   cinema
è tardi   anche

PART 2, UNIT II

UNIT III

OVERVIEW OF UNIT III

In this lesson we will really start to expand our vocabulary. We will continue to work with subject pronouns and learn a new verb, ESSERE (to be). We will learn many new expressions including professions and the days of the week. We will practice questions and answers using singular and plural verb forms and we will also be introduced to definite articles and nouns.

GRAMMAR POINTS PRESENTED

1. Answering questions negatively.
2. Questions with <u>tu</u>, <u>Lei</u> and <u>voi</u>.
3. Deleting subject pronouns.
4. The definite articles, IL, LA, I, LE
5. The Singular and Plural of Nouns: Masculine ending in O: Feminine ending in A: Masculine and Feminine ending in E.
6. The present tense of the verb ESSERE.
7. Using the expression <u>di dove</u>.

SECTION I <u>BASIC SENTENCES</u>

A. LA NUOVA MACCHINA   THE NEW CAR

Ecco il signor Fanelli.	Here's Mr. Fanelli.
È il marito di Paola.	He's Paula's husband. (lit:the husband of Paula)
Ecco la signora Fanelli.	Here's Mrs. Fanelli.
È la moglie di Carlo.	She's Carlo's wife. (lit: the wife of Carlo)
Ecco la macchina.	Here's the car.
È un'Alfa Romeo.	It's an Alfa Romeo.
È nuova e bella.	It's new and pretty.
Ecco il prezzo.	Here's the price.

NOTE: The usual abbreviations for signore, signora and signorina as Mr., Mrs., and Miss in English are:

Mr   =   sig. or signor

NOTE: (continued)

$$\text{Mrs.} = \text{Sig.}\underline{\frac{ra}{}}$$
$$\text{Miss} = \text{Sig.}\underline{\frac{na}{}}$$

Notice also the spelling of s ignor. Titles that end in
re drop the final e before a name. Titles are usually
not capitalized.

B. AL BAR	AT THE BAR
I ragazzi sono nel bar.	The boys are at the bar.
Maria è libera.	Maria is free (not busy).
Anche Gianna è libera.	Gianna is free too.
Prendono un caffè.	They have (take) coffee.

NOTE: A 'bar' in Italy is totally different from the
typical bar in the U.S. It is open from early morning
until late evening for coffee, snacks, ice-cream,soft
drinks, a glass of wine and aperitifs. It usually has
a stand-up-bar and tables both inside and outside.
Everyone, young and old, feels comfortable at a bar.

SECTION II DIALOGS

A. LA NUOVA MACCHINA	THE NEW CAR
Carlo: Paola, ho la macchina!	Paola, I have the car!
Paola: Sì, un momento.	Yes, a moment.
Carlo: Allora, ti piace?	Well, do you like it?
Paolo: È bella, veramente bellissima. Ma, il prezzo?	It's lovely, really very lovely. But the price?
Carlo: Eh,Eh,Eh, mangiamo!	Ah,Ah,Ah, let's eat.

B. AL BAR	AT THE BAR
Maria: Dove sono Mario e Gianni?	Where are Mario and Johnny?
Gianna: Nel bar.	At the bar.
Maria: Tu sei libera?	Are you free?
Gianna: Sì, sono libera.	Yes, I'm free
Maria: Allora, prendiamo un caffè con loro.	Then let's have coffee with them.

19

SECTION III   QUESTIONS
A.
1. Come si chiama il signore?   Si chiama Carlo.
2. Come si chiama la moglie?   Si chiama Paola.
3. Chi ha la macchina?   Il signore ha la macchina.
4. Com'è la macchina?   È nuova e bella.
5. Le piace? (referring to   Sì, le piace.
   Mrs. Fanelli)
6. È molto alto il prezzo?   Sì, è molto alto.
   (high, expensive)

B.
1. Dove sono i ragazzi?   I ragazzi sono nel bar.
2. Chi c'è nel bar?   I ragazzi sono nel bar.
3. È libera Maria?   Sì, è libera.
4. E Gianna?   Anche Gianna è libera.
5. Prendono Coca (Cola)   No, non prendono Coca-Cola.
6. (E) che cosa prendono?   Prendono un caffè.
NOTE: The underlined stresses pronunciation.

Disc #4 →

SECTION IV   SUPPLEMENT

A. PROFESSIONS
Io sono maestro   I'm a teacher (grade school)
       segretario   secretary
       cameriere   waiter
       commesso   clerk,salesman
       professore   teacher (H.S./college)
       avvocato   lawyer
       studente   student
       steward   steward (flight
                                           attendant)
NOTE: Most professions that refer to males end in o;
others end in e. By changing the 'o' to 'a' you may
refer to females; or in some cases drop the last letter
and add essa to form the feminine form.

Example: professore - professoressa
             avvocato   - avvocatessa
             studente   - studentessa

20

B. MISCELLANEOUS EXPRESSIONS

Gianni è occupato	Johnny's busy
stanco	tired
pronto	ready
libero	free
qui	here

NOTE: To make these feminine (except 'qui' which is invariable) change the 'o' to 'a'.
Example: Maria è occupata.

C. DAYS OF THE WEEK

I giorni della settimana sono:

lunedì	Monday
martedì	Tuesday
mercoledì	Wednesday
giovedì	Thursday
venerdì	Friday
sabato	Saturday
domenica	Sunday

Che giorno è oggi?	What day is today?
Oggi è giovedì.	Today is Thursday.

Che giorno è domani?	What day will it be tomorrow?
Domani è venerdì.	Tomorrow is Friday.

NOTE: The days of the week are not capitalized in Italian.

SECTION V ANSWERING QUESTIONS NEGATIVELY
     You are already familiar with questions that take
a 'yes' answer. To respond with 'no', and then a
negative, use no then the subject, then non followed by
the verb.

FORM: NO, SUBJECT, NON VERB

21

A. REPETITION DRILL
1. Carlo va al cinema?   No,Carlo non va al cinema.
   Is Carlo going to the   No, Carlo isn't going to
   movies?   the movies.

2. Loro vanno assieme?   No, loro non vanno assieme.
   Are they going together?   No, they're not going
                                together.

3. Carla è libera?   No, Carla non è libera.
   Is Carla free?   No, Carla's not free.

B. CUED QUESTION-ANSWER DRILL
1. Carlo va a lezione? (No)
2. I ragazzi sono nel bar? (No)
3. Loro vanno al cinema? (Sì)
4. Maria e Gianni vanno assieme? (No)

SECTION VI QUESTIONS WITH TU and LEI FORMS
        Questions with tu (You informal) and Lei (You formal)
are normally answered with Io in the same way that
questions with you (singular) in English are normally
answered with I.
Example:
English: Are you going now?   Yes, I'm going now.

Italian: Tu vai adesso?   Si, io vado adesso.

CUED QUESTION-ANSWER DRILL

1. Tu vai a lezione? (Sì)
2. Lei va adesso? (No)
3. Tu vai al bar? (Sì)
4. Lei va domani? (No)

SECTION VII QUESTIONS WITH VOI
        Questions with voi (You plural) are normally
answered with noi in the same way that questions with
you (plural) in English are normally answered with we.
Remember that this is a plural you, i.e. in the sense of
you all, or more than one person.

QUESTIONS WITH VOI (continued)

Example:

English: Are you (you and someone else) going together?
         Yes, we're going together.
Italian: Voi andate assieme?
         Si, noi andiamo assieme.

A. CUED QUESTION - ANSWER DRILL

1. Voi andate al cinema? (Sì)
2. Voi andate adesso? (No)
3. Voi andate al bar? (No, a lezione)

B. MIXED DRILL - Some of the following questions are
answered with io, others are answered with noi.

1. Tu vai al bar? (No)
2. Lei va domani? (Sì)
3. Voi andate a lezione? (Sì)
4. Tu vai al ristorante? (No, al cinema)
5. Voi andate tardi? (Sì)

C. SUBSTITUTION DRILL - In the following drill you may
practice asking questions with all of the forms of you
that we have studied: tu, Lei, and voi.

Carlo, tu vai al bar?   Signora Fanelli e Carla
Signor Fanelli,_____?   _____?
Gianni e Mario,_____?   Silvia,_____?

D. SUBSTITUTION DRILL

Paola e Mario, voi andate domani?
Sig.ra Fanelli,_____?   Silvia e Gianni,_____?
Maria,_____?   Paola,_____?

SECTION VIII SUBJECT PRONOUN DELETION
    Although it is a must to learn the subject pronouns
in Italian, and we have used them in every exercise up
to now, they are normally not used in conversation.
Since the subject is contained in the verb itself,

23

SUBJECT PRONOUN DELETION (continued)

deletion of the subject pronoun in no way changes the
meaning. Usually, they are used only for emphasis or to
avoid confusion.
Example:

Sentence with Subject:	Without Subject:
Io vado a lezione.	Vado a lezione.
I'm going to class.	I'm going to class.
Dove vai tu?	Dove vai?
Where are you going?	Where are you going?
Lui ha la macchina?	Ha la macchina?
Does he have the car?	Does he have the car?

A. Take out the subjects in the following drill.

1. Tu vai al bar.	Vai al bar.
2. Dove vanno loro?	Dove vanno?
3. Lui va adesso.	Va adesso.
4. Voi andate domani?	Andate domani?
5. Noi andiamo al ristorante.	Andiamo al ristorante.

B. Answer the following questions according to the cue
by leaving out the subject.

1. Dove vai tu? (al cinema)
2. Loro vanno domani? (Sì)
3. Voi andate? (No)
4. Lei va a lezione? (Sì)
5. Dove andate voi? (Free response)
NOTE: As in #3 when the subject is deleted, the two no
forms come together: No, non.....

SECTION IX THE GENDER OF NOUNS and DEFINITE ARTICLES
              (Singular forms)
     In Italian there are masculine and feminine nouns.
There is a large group of nouns whose singular ends in
o. These are almost always masculine nouns. Nouns whose
singular ends in a are usually feminine nouns.
EXAMPLES: masculine - ragazzo (boy)
           feminine - ragazza (girl)

24

GENDER OF NOUNS (continued)

NOTE: THE in Italian is <u>il</u> and <u>la</u>. <u>Il</u> is used with masculine nouns. <u>La</u> is used with feminine nouns.

REPETITION DRILL - SINGULAR FORMS

<u>il</u> ragazzo   <u>the</u> boy
<u>il</u> libro   <u>the</u> book
<u>la</u> ragazza   <u>the</u> girl
<u>la</u> macchina   <u>the</u> car

NOTE: IL and LA are used for almost all nouns beginning with a consonant. We will learn other forms of the definite article used with nouns beginning with vowels and other consonants later.

A. SUBSTITUTION DRILL
Il ragazzo va al bar.
____ragazza_____.   ___marito_____.
____signora_____.   ___signorina_____.

B. SUBSTITUTION DRILL
Ecco il marito.
_____libro.   _____ragazzo.
_____macchina.   _____signora.

C. SUBSTITUTION DRILL
Ecco la ragazza. _4 - 1620_
_____signora.   _____signorina.
_____marito.   _____libro.
_____macchina.   _____prezzo.
_____ragazzo.

REPETITION DRILL - MASCULINE PLURAL FORMS
     To make a masculine noun plural in Italian you change the last letter <u>o</u> to <u>i</u>. Unlike English there is a 'the' plural; therefore, <u>il</u> simply becomes <u>i</u>.

EXAMPLES

Singular: Plural:
il ragazzo - the boy   i ragazzi - the boys
il libro - the book   i libri - the books
il marito - the husband   i mariti- the husbands

REPETITION DRILL - FEMININE PLURAL FORMS
     To make a feminine noun-which ends in a in the
singular- plural,you change the last letter a to e.
La becomes le for the plural.
                    EXAMPLES
Singular: Plural:
la ragazza - the girl   le ragazze - the girls
la macchina - the car   le macchine - the cars
la signora - the lady   le signore - the ladies

D. SUBSTITUTION DRILL (Plural forms)
I mariti vanno adesso.
____ragazze_____.   ____ragazzi_____.
____macchine_____.   ____signore_____.

NOTE: Remember that if the subject is plural, just as
in English the verb must also be plural.

E. MIXED SUBSTITUTION DRILL (all forms of 'the': il, i,
                            la, le)
Dove va il ragazzo?
_____signora?   _____mariti?
_____macchine?   _____ragazze?
_____ragazza?   _____signorine?

REPETITION DRILL - NOUNS THAT END IN 'E'
     There are some nouns in Italian that end in e. They
may be either masculine or feminine. Therefore, you
must learn their gender; that is,whether they are masculine or feminine. The word the for each will tell you
this.
     Examples: il ristorante
                la lezione
The plural of nouns ending in e is i for both masculine
and feminine.
     Examples: i ristoranti   the restaurants
                le lezioni   the classes

F. SUBSTITUTION DRILL (double item)
Ecco la lezione.
_____le_____.
_____ristorante.
_____i_____.

SECTION X VERB ESSERE - TO BE

Essere is an irregular verb in Italian as is andare. You have already been introduced to most of the forms of essere in the present tense. Learn its forms and their English meanings.

A. REPETITION DRILL

Io sono nel bar.	I'm at the bar.
Tu sei nel bar.	You are at the bar.
Lei (formale) è nel bar.	You (formal) are at the bar.
Lei è nel bar.	She is at the bar.
Lui è nel bar.	He is at the bar.
Noi siamo nel bar.	We are at the bar.
Voi siete nel bar.	You are at the bar.
Loro sono nel bar.	They are at the bar.

NOTE: Io and loro have the same form.

B. SUBSTITUTION DRILL
Mario è qui.
Tu_____.   Loro_____.   Voi_____.

C. SUBSTITUTION DRILL
Io sono nel ristorante.
Maria ed io_____.   Lui_____.
Lei (formale) _____.

D. CUED QUESTION-ANSWER DRILL USING ESSERE
1. Che ora è? (3:15)
2. Dov'è Mario? (nel bar)
3. Tu sei libero(a)?   (Sì)
4. Siete a lezione? (No)
5. Lei è studente? (Sì)
6. Sei pronta? (No)
7. Dove sono le ragazze?   (nel ristorante)
8. Che giorno è oggi?   (martedì)
9. Chi c'è? (Gianni)
10. È bella la macchina?   (Sì)

27

E. WHERE PEOPLE ARE FROM - REPETITION DRILL

Di dove è Lei?   Where are you from?
Di dove sei tu?   Where are you from?
                                (lit: from where are you)

Io sono italiano.   I am Italian.
Io sono americano.   I am American.

NOTE: Di dove is an interrogative expression that may
be used to ask where a person is from (origin,nationality).
It is used with essere.

F. FORMING QUESTIONS (Not recorded)
      Make up 7 different questions using all of the forms
of essere and have another person answer them.

SECTION XI REVIEW QUESTIONS (Not recorded)

1. Dove vanno i ragazzi?
2. Sei professoressa?
3. Com'è la macchina?
4. Che giorno è domani?
5. È libera Maria?
6. E tu?
7. Le signore prendono caffè o Coca-cola?
8. Come si chiama il marito di Paola?
9. Ti piace il bar?
10.Sei stanco(a)?
11.Mario è avvocato?
12.Di dove sei tu?
13.Mario è italiano?
14.È nuova la macchina?
15.Siete a lezione?

SECTION XII LEARNING ACTIVITIES

1. In the following exercise make different complete
sentences using the verbs given. Compose them using as
many masculine and feminine nouns in the singular and
plural as possible.
a.____sono_____.   d.____va_____.
b.____vanno_____.   e.____sono____.
c.____è_____.   f.____vanno___.

28

LEARNING ACTIVITIES (continued)

g.____è____.   h.____va_____.

2. Find a picture of a man, a woman and a car in a
magazine. Describe them using as much supplementary
vocabulary as possible.

3. Section VII, Substitution Drill D: complete the drill
and then answer the questions

4. Interview another person in Italian and find out
his/her profession, a miscellaneous expression about
him/her (busy, tired, etc., from Section IV), if he/she
has a car and where he/she is going now. Be prepared
to introduce him/her using Si chiama (name). You may
add other vocabulary if you wish.

PART 2, UNIT III

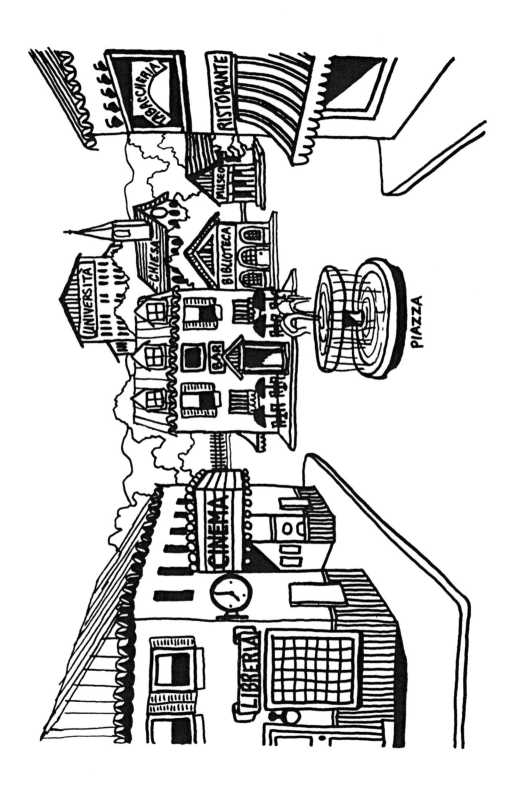

UNIT IV

OVERVIEW OF UNIT IV

In this unit we will concentrate on the vocabulary of food and places. We will work with contractions and review question words. The verb <u>avere</u> (to have) will be explained and we will continue definite articles and nouns. Also, in this lesson the verbs we have learned so far will be reviewed and some common points of most verbs will be stressed.

GRAMMAR POINTS PRESENTED

1. Contractions with 'a' (al, alla, ai, alle).
2. 'a' in time expressions.
3. Present tense of verb AVERE (to have).
4. General rules for verbs in the present tense.
5. The definite articles <u>lo</u> and <u>gli</u>.
6. The singular and plural of nouns that begin with other consonants (z or s+a consonant).
7. The singular and plural of nouns that begin with vowels.
8. The plural of nouns ending in -<u>io</u>.
9. The plural of nouns ending in -<u>co</u>, -<u>ca</u> and -<u>go</u>, -<u>ga</u>.
10. Using question words.

SECTION I <u>BASIC</u> <u>SENTENCES</u>

A. IL PRANZO - PT. 1	LUNCH - PT 1
Cinzia ed Antonio sono studenti.	Cynthia and Anthony are students.
Sono anch'amici.	They're also friends.
Cinzia ha fame.	Cynthia is hungry(has hunger)
Antonio è fortunato.	Anthony is lucky.
Ha soldi.	He has money.
Vanno alla tavola calda.	They go to a quick service restaurant.(hot table)
Il vino è ottimo.	The wine is great.

32

B. IL PRANZO - PT. 2   LUNCH - PT. 2
Mangiano il pranzo.   They eat lunch.
Il primo piatto è   The first course is
 "tagliatelle"   "tagliatelle" (macaroni)
C'è vino rosso.   There's red wine.
La lezione è alle tre.   Class is at three.
Hanno tempo.   They have time.

SECTION II DIALOGS

A. IL PRANZO-PT. 1   LUNCH-PT. 1
Cinzia: Ho fame.   I'm hungry.
Antonio: Anch'io.   So am I.
Cinzia: Dove mangiamo?   Where do we eat? At the
 Alla mensa o alla tavola   cafeteria or the quick
 calda?   service?
Antonio: Oggi, sono   Today I'm lucky (in luck).
 fortunato. Ho soldi.   I have money.
Cinzia: Bene. Allora   Good. Then let's go to the
 andiamo alla Vecchia   "Little Old Stove".
 Fornarina.
Antonio: Si. Hanno un   Yes, they have a great wine!
 ottimo vino.

NOTE: Sometimes a tavola calda is translated as cafeteria.
However, although it is a quick service restaurant, you
are still waited on rather than picking up the food
yourself.

The mensa is the university or company cafeteria.

B. IL PRANZO-PT. 2   LUNCH-PT. 2
Antonio: Che cosa   What shall we have? (take)
 prendiamo?
Cinzia: Per me un bel pranzo. For me, a nice lunch. For
 Come primo piatto -   the first course,tagliatelle.
 tagliatelle. Come secondo- For the second-a mixed
 arrosto misto-come contorno grill. As a side dish
 pomodori al forno e   baked tomatoes and salad.
 insalata. Poi frutta e   Then fruit and coffee.
 caffè.
Antonio: Oh si, abbiamo   Oh yes, we have time.
 tempo. La lezione è   Class is at three.
 alle tre.

33

IL PRANZO (continued)

| Cinzia: E un mezzo litro di vino rosso! | And a half liter of red wine! |

NOTE: Il pranzo is the big meal of the day and in most parts of Italy it is still eaten in a leisurely fashion (with two courses and a side dish). Almost everything closes at lunch time in Italy including the university. Usually 12:30-3:00 or 3:30 is reserved for eating and resting. Most stores close for most of the afternoon and reopen at 5:00. Stores then stay open until 7:30 or 8:00.

SECTION III QUESTIONS

A.
1. Sono professori Cinzia ed Antonio?   No, sono studenti.
2. Ha fame Cinzia?   Sì, ha fame.
3. Dove mangiano?   Mangiano alla tavola calda.
4. Chi è fortunato?   Antonio è fortunato.
5. Perché?(why)   Ha soldi.
6. Dove vanno?   Vanna alla Vecchia Fornarina.
7. È un McDonald's?   No, non è un McDonald's.
8. Com'è il vino?   Il vino è ottimo.

B.
1. Che cosa prende Cinzia come primo piatto?   Prende tagliatelle.
2. Che cosa prende con il caffè?   Prende frutta.
3. Hanno tempo?   Sì, hanno tempo.
4. A che ora è la lezione?   La lezione è alle tre.
5. Prendono una Coca(cola)?   No, prendono un mezzo litro di vino rosso.

SECTION IV SUPPLEMENT-MEALS
A. I pasti sono:
   (The)meals are:

la colazione	breakfast
il pranzo	lunch
la cena	dinner

34

B. Per colazione c'è: For breakfast there's:
    caffè (liscio)   coffee (plain)
    cappuccino con schiuma   cappuccino with foam or
     o panna   whipped cream
    caffè macchiato   coffee with milk
    latte maccniato   milk with coffee
    cornetti   crescent rolls
    paste   pastries
    biscotti   biscuits (cookies)

   Al bar ci sono anche: At the bar there are also:
    il gelato   ice cream
    gli snacks   snacks
    i panini   sandwiches
    gli aperitivi   aperitifs

NOTE: gli snacks is an 'americanism', but you will see
it and hear it at a bar.

C. PLACES TO GO
    Dove vai?   Where are you going?
    Vado: I'm going:

    al parco   to the park
    al centro   downtown
    al museo   to the museum
    al negozio   to the store
    al giardino   to the garden
    al teatro   to the theater
    al cinema   to the movies
    al circolo   to the student center

Dove andate?   Where are you going?
Andiamo: We're going:
    alla discoteca   to the disco
    alla biblioteca   to the library
    alla mensa   to the cafeteria
    *a scuola   to school
    *a lezione   to class
NOTE: *No definite article needed.

PLACES TO GO (continued)

Dove vanno le signore?	Where are the ladies going?
Vanno:	They are going:
*in chiesa	to church
in casa	home
in libreria	to the bookstore
in ufficio	to the office
in albergo	to the hotel

NOTE: *Note use of in with these specific words.

Here is a very useful expression:
Me ne vado.   I'm going (I'm leaving)

D. FREE CONVERSATION

Antonio: Cinzia, dove vai?   Cinzia: Al centro.
Antonio: E dopo?   Cinzia: Al parco.
Antonio: E dopo?   Cinzia: Alla mensa.

E. Make up your own answers to the questions.(Not recorded)

Dove vai?
E dopo?

SECTION V CONTRACTIONS WITH 'A'

As you saw in Places to Go, Supplement section C,
you can contract the word a (to) and the definite article
the in Italian.

Before masculine singular nouns a il contracts or
combines to form al (al museo).

Before feminine singular nouns a la becomes alla
(alla mensa).

Before masculine plural nouns a and i are simply
connected to form ai (ai musei).

Before feminine plural nouns a and le become alle
(alle mense).

36

A. REPETITION DRILL

Antonio va al museo.	Anthony is going to the museum.
Antonio va alla mensa.	Anthony is going to the cafeteria.
Antonio va ai musei.	Anthony is going to the museums.
Antonio va alle mense.	Anthony is going to the cafeterias.

B. SUBSTITUTION DRILL

Antonio va al negozio.
_____giardino.　　　　　_____mensa.
_____biblioteca

C. SINGULAR MIXED FORM DRILL - AL, ALLA, IN

Vanno alla discoteca.
_____albergo.　　　　　_____cinema.
_____lezione.　　　　　_____chiesa.

D. SUBSTITUTION DRILL PLURAL FORMS

I ragazzi vanno alle mense.
_____lezioni.　　　　　_____parchi.*
_____biblioteche.*　　　_____negozi.*

*These plural forms are explained in Section IX.

SECTION VI 'A' IN TIME EXPRESSIONS

　　　In time expressions a (to) means at.　Study the following examples.

A che ora vanno al centro?	(At) what time are they going downtown?
Vanno al centro:	They are going downtown:
all'una	at 1:00
alle tre	at 3:00
alle cinque	at 5:00
a mezzogiorno	at noon
a mezzanotte	at midnight

NOTE: Remember the 'a' does not tell time, it states at what time you are doing something or something is happening.

A. REPETITION DRILL

Andiamo all'una.	Let's go at 1:00
Andiamo all'una del pomeriggio.	Let's go at 1:00 in the afternoon.
Andiamo alle otto.	Let's go at 8:00.
Andiamo alle otto della mattina.(or:di mattina)	Let's go at 8:00 in the morning.
Andiamo alle sette.	Let's go at 7:00.
Andiamo alle sette di sera.	Let's go at 7:00 in the evening.
Andiamo a mezzogiorno.	Let's go at noon.

B. CUED QUESTION-ANSWER DRILL

1. A che ora vai a lezione? (at 6:00)
2. A che ora va il ragazzo? (at 1:30)
3. A che ora avete lezione? (at 4:00 on the dot)
4. A che ora vanno al cinema? (at 8:00 in the evening)
5. A che ora va Mario? (at 9:00)

SECTION VII THE IRREGULAR VERB AVERE

You have already been introduced to most of the forms of the verb avere - to have. Learn its forms and their English meanings. Subject pronouns are included in parenthesis, since from now on they will be used normally for emphasis or to avoid confusion.

A. REPETITION DRILL

(io) ho soldi	I have money
(tu) hai soldi	You have money
(Lei) ha soldi	You have money
(lei) ha soldi	She has money
(lui) ha soldi	He has money
(noi) abbiamo soldi	We have money
(voi) avete soldi	You have money
(loro) hanno soldi	They have money

B. SUBSTITUTION DRILL - Cinzia ha fame.

Mario _____.   La signora_____.
I ragazzi_____.   Tu_____.

C. SUBSTITUTION DRILL
Giovanni ha i libri.

Loro_____ .   Carla e Mario_____ .
Gianni ed io_____ .   I signori_____ .

D. CUED QUESTION-ANSWER DRILL
1. Tu hai il libro o il caffè? (caffè)
2. Il signor Fanelli ha la macchina? (sì)
3. Dove avete lezioni? (a BCC)
4. Le ragazzi hanno lezione adesso? (sì)
5. Chi ha fame? (Mario)
6. Ha fame Lei? (sì)

E. Make up four (4) questions to ask another person using the verb avere. (Not recorded)

SECTION VIII GENERAL RULES FOR VERBS
     We have learned three verbs so far: andare (to go).
essere (to be), and avere (to have). Although they are
irregular verbs, fortunately they have certain things
in common among themselves and with most verbs in Italian
in the present tense. Study the following general rules.

A. 1. Verbs end in the sound and letter o in the
      io or I form: vado - sono - ho

   2. Verbs end in the sound and letter i in the tu
      or you informal form: vai - sei - hai

   3. Verbs end in a vowel and vowel sound (a,e,and
      sometimes o) in the Lei(formale), lei and lui,
      or you formal, she and he forms:
      va - è - ha

   4.   Verbs end in iamo in the noi or we form.
      andiamo - siamo - abbiamo

   5. Verbs end in te in the voi or you plural form.
      andate - siete - avete

   6. Verbs end in no in the loro or they form.
      vanno - sono - hanno *

39

GENERAL RULES FOR VERBS (continued)

NOTE: * A few verbs, normally irregular ones, double the 'n' and you should remember this.

B. COMPLETION DRILL (Not recorded)
   Complete the following as per example:

1. Io vado
     son_
     h_

2. Noi abbiamo
     and____
     s_____

3. Tu hai
     va_
     se_

4. Loro vanno
     han_
     so_

5. Lei è
     h_
     v_

6. Voi avete
     anda_
     sie_

SECTION IX OTHER DEFINITE ARTICLES AND OTHER NOUNS
   As you have already learned, most nouns beginning with a consonant take il and la as the definite article the. There are some other nouns that take other forms. Study the following examples:

lo zio   - the uncle   gli zii*   - the uncles
lo studente- the student   gli studenti - the students
lo stadio   -the stadium   gli stadi*   - the stadiums

1. When a masculine noun begins with z or s followed by a consonant (called 's impure' in Italian) its form is lo in the singular and gli in the plural. (Feminine forms are regular)
   *Nouns ending in io become ii in the plural if the i is stressed, as in lo zio. Otherwise, the ending is simply i as in stadio and negozio which become stadi and negozi.

A. REPETITION DRILL
Lo zio è nel bar.
*Gli zii sono nel bar.
Lo studente è nel bar.
Gli studenti sono nel bar.
Gli spaghetti sono nel bar.

NOTE:*If you have any problem with this sound, go back to the pronunciation tape and turn to Exercise 10 ('g' sounds) in your Introductory Unit.

40

2. When a _masculine_ or _feminine_ noun begins with a vowel
the definite article is l' in the singular. In the
plural gli is used with the masculine and le with the
feminine. Study the following examples:

l' amico   - the friend   gli amici   - the friends
l' albergo - the hotel   *gli alberghi - the hotels
l' amica   - the friend   *le amiche   - the friends
NOTE: Masculine nouns that end in -go normally become
-ghi in the plural. (Ex: albergo, alberghi) Masculine
nouns that end in -co become -chi in the plural if the
stress falls on the next to the last syllable. (Ex: parco
parchi) One of the several exceptions to this stress
rule is amico, amici. Nouns ending in -co whose stress
is on any other syllable normally form the plural in -ci
(medico, medici)
        Feminine nouns that end in -ca or -ga become -che
or -ghe respectively in the plural (biblioteca,biblioteche,
bottega(shop), botteghe).

A. REPETITION DRILL
        L'amico è qui.
        Gli amici sono qui.
        L'albergo è qui.
        Gli alberghi sono qui.
        L'amica è qui.
        Le amiche sono qui.

B. SUBSTITUTION DRILL - lo, l', gli, le
Ecco lo stadio!
_____amico!   _____studente!
_____alberghi!   _____amici!
_____amica!   _____amiche!
_____stadi!

C. TRANSFORMATION DRILL - Change the following form from
singular to plural or plural to singular.
Examples: Ecco le amiche!   Ecco l'amica!
           Ecco lo stadio!   Ecco gli stadi!
1. Ecco l'amico!   Ecco _____
2. Ecco gli studenti!   _____
3. Ecco lo spaghetto!   _____
4. Ecco lo zio!   _____

41

TRANSFORMATION DRILL (continued)

5. Ecco gli alberghi!   _____.

D. MIXED DRILL - Be sure to review all definite article
forms in Units III and IV before doing this drill.

Dove sono i libri?
_____amici?   _____lezione?
_____ragazza?   _____negozi?
_____studente?   _____signorina?
_____zii?   _____amiche?
_____macchine?

SECTION X QUESTION WORD REVIEW
        We have used four question words so far: come - how
and what; dove - where; chi - who; che - what. Using
question words is very simple in Italian, since as in
English they begin the sentence. Come and dove and chi are
followed by the verb and then by the subject in a
sentence. Study the examples.

Come sta la ragazza?   How is the girl?
Dove va Mario?   Where's Mario going?
Chi ha la macchina?   Who has the car?
Che ora è?   What time is it?
Come ti chiami?   What's your name?
*Dov'è il marito?   Where's the husband?
*Com'è il vino?   How's the wine?
NOTE: *When dove and come are followed by the verb form
è, the last 'e' on each contracts to form dov'è and com'è.

A. TRANSFORMATION DRILL - The following are answers.
Using the underlined word as a cue, write questions with
the appropriate question word:
Example:
        Il ragazzo va a lezione.   (Answer)
        Chi va a lezione?   (Question)

1. Lo studente va a scuola.   _____?
2. Sono le tre.   _____?
3. Maria sta benissimo.   _____?
4. I signori hanno la macchina.   _____?

42

TRANSFORMATION DRILL (continued)

5. Mi chiamo <u>Elena</u>. _____?
6. Vado in <u>albergo</u>. _____?

SECTION XI <u>REVIEW QUESTIONS</u> (Not recorded)
1. A che ora hai lezione?
2. Dove sono le ragazza?
3. Mario, hai soldi?
4. Dove vanno gli studenti?
5. Come sta il signor Palmieri?
6. Sei studente (studentessa)?
7. E dopo, dove andate?
8. Chi va alla mensa?
9. Chi c'è nel bar?
10. Dove va lo zio?
11. Chi è l'amica di Carlo?
12. Com'è il vino?
13. Sono amici Antonio e Cinzia?
14. Hanno fame gli studenti?
15. E tu, hai fame?
16. Che cosa prende Luciana?
17. Avete tempo?
18. Dove mangiano?
19. Andate alla tavola calda o in pizzeria?
20. Sei fortunato(a)?
21. Ti piace il contorno?
22. (Answer with a plural noun) Vai alla biblioteca?
23. (Answer with a plural noun) Vanno al parco?
24. Dove vanno? (Answer with a plural noun)

SECTION XII <u>LEARNING ACTIVITIES</u>
1. Answer the following questions:
   a. Tina è la zia. Ed Antonio? _____
   b. Gianni è l'amico. E Carla?_____
   c. Marco e Carlo sono studenti?   E Paolo?_____

2. Compose questions for the following answers using the underlined word as a cue. Use these questions words: <u>come</u>, <u>dove</u>, <u>chi</u>, <u>che</u>.
Example: Answer: La ragazza sta <u>bene</u>.
          Question:Come sta la ragazza?

43

LEARNING ACTIVITIES (continued)

2.(cont.)
a. Si chiama Mario. _____?
b. La moglie va in chiesa. _____?
c. Andiamo in albergo. _____?
d. Sono le otto. _____?
e. Cinzia non sta bene. _____?
f. Maria è fortunata. _____?

3. Supply the missing verb in each sentence. It must be
a logical choice. (There may be more than one logical
choice)
a. Chi_____fame?
b. Dove_____la ragazza?
c. Gli studenti_____in pizzeria.
d. Il signor Fanelli_____soldi.
e. Noi_____fortunati.
f. Come_____la moglie?

4. Write an original story of about five lines about two
students who decide to have lunch. Remember, this is
a story (written in the third person), not a conversation.
Use your imagination.

5. Match column A with column B.

A	B
a. zio	a. macchiato
b. colazione	b. cornetti
c. 8:00	c. pomodori al forno
d. caffè	d. Cinzia
e. contorno	e. ora
f. circolo	f. studenti
g. studentessa	g. lo

6. From among the following places, select the one that
best completes each sentence. Make sure to use the
proper form of to: discoteca, tavola calda, teatro,
scuola, ufficio, albergo, casa.
a. Ho fame; vado_____   d. C'è Hamlet; vado_____
b. Sono studente; vado____   e. Sono avvocato; vado_____
c. Mi piace ballare(dance);
     vado_____.

PART 2, UNIT IV

OVERVIEW OF UNIT V
        In this unit we will really begin to use and manip-
ulate the Italian language as we learn our first large
group of regular verbs, the -are group. A great deal of
vocabulary will be introduced including exclamations,
places to go and directions.

GRAMMAR POINTS PRESENTED
        1. Contractive forms of'a'(all', allo, agli,alle).
        2. The present tense of regular -are verbs.
           (included are -care,-gare,-ciare,-giare verbs)
        3. The polite command form of -are verbs.

SECTION I BASIC SENTENCES

A. ALL'UNIVERSITÀ

AT THE UNIVERSITY

C'è una bella ragazza.
There's a pretty girl.

È l'amica della sorella di
Carla.
She's Carla's sister's friend
(lit:the friend of the
 sister of Carla).

Parlano con la sorella di
Carla.
They speak with Carla's
sister.

Gianni *necessita aiuto.
Johnny needs help.

NOTE: * Stress for pronunciation. The verb necessitare
is used here to indicate 'need' since in this unit we are
presenting -are verbs. It is also a good verb to practice
stress and pronunciation.Another expression,aver bisogno
(di) is normally used to indicate 'need'. It will be used
in Unit VI.

B. DOVE SI TROVA...?

WHERE IS...?

Un signore cerca il Davide.
A gentleman is looking for
the David.

Parla con una signorina.
He speaks with a young lady.

Si trova all'Accademia.
It's at(is found)the Academy.

Non è lontano.
It's not far.

Ci arriva subito.
One gets there quickly.

Gira a sinistra.
He turns left.

Continua diritto.
He continues straight ahead.

È sulla destra.
It's on the right.

46

SECTION II DIALOGS

A. ALL'UNIVERSITÀ | AT THE UNIVERSITY

Gianni: Mamma mia! Che
bella ragazza! | Wow! What a pretty girl.

Carla: Studia storia. È
l'amica di mia sorella. | She studies history. She's
my sister's friend.

Gianni: Benissimo! Parliamo
con tua sorella. | Great! Let's talk to your
sister.

Carla: Senti, necessiti
aiuto in storia? | Say, do you need help in
history?

Gianni: Senz'altro,
necessito aiuto in tutto! | Of course, I need help in
everything!

B. DOVE SI TROVA...? | WHERE IS...?

Un signore: Scusi, dove si
trova il Davide di
Michelangelo? | Excuse me, where is(is found)
Michelangelo's David?

Una signorina: Non è lontano
da qui. Si trova all'
Accademia delle Belle Arti. | It's not far from here. It's
(found) at the Academy of
Fine Arts.

Un signore: Bene. Come ci
arrivo? | Good, How do I get there?
(arrive there)

Una signorina:All'angolo
giri a sinistra e continui
diritto. È subito sulla
destra. | At the corner, turn left
and continue straight ahead.
It's just (quickly) on the
right.

NOTE: The Academy of Fine Arts where the David is located
is found in the city of Florence. It is actually called
the Galleria dell'Accademia.

SECTION II QUESTIONS

A. ALL'UNIVERSITÀ | AT THE UNIVERSITY
1. Com'è la ragazza? | La ragazza è bella.
2. Che cosa studia? | Studia storia.
3. Con chi parlano? | Parlano con la sorella di
Carla.
4. Gianni necessita aiuto? | Sì, necessita aiuto.
5. In che cosa? | Necessita aiuto in tutto!

B. DOVE SI TROVA..? | WHERE IS...?
1. Che cosa cerca il
signore? | Cerca il Davide di
Michelangelo.

47

DOVE SI TROVA...? (continued)

2. Con chi parla?   Parla con una signorina.
3. Dov'è Il Davide?   Il Davide si trova All'
                                   Accademia delle Belle Arti.
4. È lontano?   No, non è lontano.
5. Ci arriva subito?   Sì, ci arriva subito.
6. Come ci arriva?   Gira a sinistra e continua
                                   diritto.

SECTION IV SUPPLEMENT
A.SOME USEFUL EXCLAMATIONS!
1. Mamma Mia!   Wow, say, oh boy, etc.
                                   (lit: My mother)
2. Per carità!   Please (don't mention it)
                                   Don't be ridiculous!
3. Accidenti!   Darn it, damn it.
4. Porca miseria!   "   "   "   "
5. *Mannaggia!   "   "   "   "
6. Maledizione!   "   "   "   "
7. Va via!   Go away!

NOTE: * MANNAGGIA - although some dictionaries may not
contain it, it is a word you will hear and so we include
it here.

B. MORE PLACES TO GO
Dove vai?
        Vado all'università   To the university
             all'opera   To the opera
             all'ospedale   To the hospital
             all'Accademia   To the academy
               (art museum)
             allo stadio   To the stadium

C. WHERE IS.....?
        Dov'è....
        Dove si trova...
          *il gabinetto?   the restroom
           il bagno   the bathroom
           la toiletta   the toilet
           l'ufficio postale   the post office
           la tabaccheria   the tabacco shop(stationery)

48

WHERE IS.....? (continued)

NOTE: * il gabinetto can also be an office such as that
of a doctor, lawyer, etc.

D. WHY AND BECAUSE

Cinzia: Vado all'opera stasera.(I'm going to the opera
                                 tonight.)
*Antonio: Perché? (Why)
Cinzia: Perché mi piace molto! (Because I like it a lot!)
NOTE: *Perché means both why and because. There is no
change in spelling.

SECTION V FREE CONVERSATION (Not recorded)
     Make up and write out five short conversations like
D in Section IV, using perché for why and because. You
may use any and all of the verbs learned so far.

SECTION VI MORE CONTRACTIONS WITH A
     As you saw in Suppliment, Section IV, 'a' also
contracts with words that begin with vowels and 's' +
a consonant.

1. Before masculine and feminine singular nouns beginning
with a vowel, a + l becomes all'.

2. Before masculine singular nouns beginning with z or
s + a consonant, a + lo contracts to allo.

3. Before masculine plural nouns that begin with a vowel
or z or s + a consonant, a + gli simply combine to form
agli.

4. Before feminine plural nouns that begin with a vowel,
a + le becomes alle. (The form is alle for all feminine
plural nouns.)

A. REPETITION DRILL - Study and repeat the following
examples:
Andiamo all'università.   We're going to the university.
*Andiamo alle università.   We're going to the university.

49

REPETITION DRILL (continued)

Andiamo allo stadio.   We're going to the stadium.
Andiamo agli stadi.   We're going to the stadiums.
Andiamo all'ospedale.   We're going to the hospital.
Andiamo agli ospedali.   We're going to the hospitals.

NOTE:*Nouns ending in an accented vowel in the singular
remain the same in the plural.
Example:
          la città   le città
          l'università   le università

B. SUBSTITUTION DRILL (Singular forms)
I ragazzi vanno allo stadio.
_____università.
_____ospedale.
_____opera.

C. SUBSTITUTION DRILL (Plural forms)
Vado agli stadi.
_____università.
_____opere.
_____ospedali.

D. SUBSTITUTION DRILL (Mixed forms)
Una signorina va all'università.
_____ospedale.
_____stadio.
_____università (plural)

SECTION VII REGULAR -ARE VERBS
     There is a large group of verbs in Italian that end
in -are in the infinitive (to.....) or basic form. They
are called regular -are verbs because they all follow
the same pattern in deriving their forms. Also, they
follow the generalizations as outlined in Unit IV, so
forming them in the present tense is a simple process.
Study the following list of regular -are verbs.

lavorare   to work   abitare   to live
studiare   to study   aspettare   to wait for
parlare   to speak   tornare   to return

-ARE VERBS (continued)

necessitare	to need	ritornare	to return
trovare	to find	spiegare*	to explain
continuare	to continue	cercare*	to look for
girare	to turn	mangiare**	to eat
arrivare	to arrive		

NOTE: To find the stem (which contains the meaning) to which you add the present tense endings, you drop the -are from the infinitive:

Infinitive	Stem
parlare	parl
studiare	studi

NOTE: For the various subjects below you must add the endings indicated in the ending column.

Example: parlare

Subject	Stem	Ending	Typical Sentence
io...	parl...	o	(Io) parlo molto.
tu...	parl...	i	(Tu) parli molto.
Lei...	parl...	a	(Lei) parla molto.
lui...	parl...	a	(Lui) parla molto.
lei...	parl...	a	(Lei) parla molto.
noi...	parl...	iamo	(Noi) parliamo molto.
voi...	parl...	ate	(Voi) parlate molto.
loro..	parl...	ano	(Loro) parlano molto.

REMEMBER that a typical Italian sentence in the present tense can have several meanings.

(Io) studio.	I study, I do study, I am studying.
(Tu) studi?	Do you study, are you studying?

REMEMBER too, that there are no special helping verbs like do or doesn't. Do not try to translate do or does. This also applies to are, is and am for the moment.

A. REPETITION DRILL

Io parlo italiano.	I speak Italian.
Tu parli italiano.	You speak Italian.

REPETITION DRILL (continued)

Lei parla italiano.	You speak Italian.
Lui parla italiano.	He speaks Italian.
Lei parla italiano.	She speaks Italian.
Noi parliamo italiano.	We speak Italian.
Voi parlate italiano.	You speak Italian.
Loro parlano italiano.	They speak Italian.

NOTE:*Verbs ending in -care (cercare) and -gare (spiegare) add h in the tu and noi forms before the ending. This is done to keep the hard sound of the c and g as in the infinitive.

EXAMPLES:

io cerco	noi cerchiamo
tu cerchi	voi cercate
io spiego	noi spieghiamo
tu spieghi	voi spiegate

NOTE:** Verbs ending in -ciare and -giare (mangiare) drop the i of their stem in the tu and noi forms. The same is true of studiare.

B. REPETITION DRILL

(Io) cerco il libro.	I look for the book.
(Tu) cerchi il libro.	You look for the book.
(Lei) cerca il libro.	You(formal)look for the book.
(Lui) cerca il libro.	He looks for the book.
(Lei) cerca il libro.	She looks for the book.
(Noi) cerchiamo il libro.	We look for the book.
(Voi) cercate il libro.	You look for the book.
(Loro) cercano il libro.	They look for the book.

C. REPETITION DRILL

(Io) spiego la lezione.	I explain the lesson.
(Tu) spieghi la lezione.	You explain the lesson.
(Lei) spiega la lezione.	You(formal)explain the lesson.
(Lui) spiega la lezione.	He explains the lesson.
(Lei) spiega la lezione.	She explains the lesson.
(Noi) spieghiamo la lezione.	We explain the lesson.

REPETITION DRILL (continued)

(Voi) spiegate la lezione.   You explain the lesson.
(Loro) spiegano la lezione.   They explain the lesson.

D. REPETITION DRILL
(Io) mangio il pranzo.   I eat lunch.
(Tu) mangi il pranzo.   You eat lunch.
(Lei) mangia il pranzo.   You eat lunch.
(Lui) mangia il pranzo.   He eats lunch.
(Lei) mangia il pranzo.   She eats lunch.
(Noi) mangiamo il pranzo.   We eat lunch.
(Voi) mangiate il pranzo.   You eat lunch.
(Loro) mangiano il pranzo.   They eat lunch.

E. SUBSTITUTION DRILL
Gina studia storia.
Lei (formale)_____   Noi_____
Tu_____   Io_____
Lei_____   Voi_____

F. SUBSTITUTION DRILL
Loro non lavorano domani.
Noi_____   Io_____
Gianni ed io_____   Lui_____
Il ragazzo_____   Tu_____

G. SUBSTITUTION DRILL
Il signore gira a destra.
Io_____   Loro_____
Maria_____   Voi_____
Maria e Roberto_____   Lei (formale)_____

H. SUBSTITUTION DRILL
Mario cerca un libro.
Tu_____   Voi_____
Gina ed io_____   Lui_____
Loro_____   I ragazzi_____

I. REPETITION DRILL   J. QUESTION-ANSWER DRILL
Il signore cerca una   1. Che cosa cerca il
liberia.   signore?

I. REPETITION DRILL (con't)   J. QUESTION-ANSWER DRILL
                                   (con't.)

Gira a destra.   2. Gira a sinistra?
Parla con una signorina.   3. Con chi parla?

K. REPETITION DRILL   L. QUESTION-ANSWER DRILL
I ragazzi studiano a scuola. 1. Dove studiano i ragazzi?
Non parlano italiano.   2. Parlano italiano?
Arrivano tardi.   3. Arrivano subito?

M. REPETITION DRILL   N. QUESTION-ANSWER DRILL
Io non parlo italiano.   1. Tu parli italiano?
Studio italiano.   2. Che cosa studi tu?
Necessito aiuto!   3. Che cosa necessiti?

O. REPETITION DRILL   P. QUESTION-ANSWER DRILL
Non abitiamo lontano.   1. Abitate lontano?
Ritorniamo a casa.   2. Dove ritornate?
Mangiamo un gelato.   3. Che cosa mangiate?

Q. MIXED QUESTION-ANSWER DRILL
1. Che parlano loro?   (italiano)
2. Dove lavori?   (nel bar)
3. A che ora arriva la ragazza?   (alle tre)
4. Spiegate la lezione?   (sì)
5. Aspettano la macchina?   (no)
6. Che cosa cercate?   (i soldi)
7. Studi molto?   (sì)
8. Continuano diritto i signori?   (no)
9. Che necessita Gianni?   (aiuto)
10. Abiti nel New Jersey?   (sì)
11. Che cosa mangiano gli studenti?   (la pizza)
12. Il marito ritorna in ufficio?   (no, a casa)

SECTION VIII QUESTIONS   (Not recorded)
     Make up 10 questions in Italian using all the forms
of the -are verbs that you have studied here. Be sure
to practice writing the verbs that have some spelling
changes.

SECTION IX POLITE COMMAND FORM

As you know, in the Dialog "Dove si trova", the Polite (Lei formale) Command or Imperative form of regular -are verbs ends in i. It is the same word as the 'tu' form of the verb. EXAMPLE - parli - speak! In commands no subject pronoun is used.

		LEI	
VERB	STEM	COMMAND FORM	ENGLISH MEANING
aspettare	aspett	aspetti	wait!
parlare	parl	parli	speak!
girare	gir	giri	turn!
continuare	continu	continui	continue!

A. GIVE THE LEI(FORMALE) command of the following verbs in Italian: (Not recorded)
1. tornare
2. parlare
3. mangiare
4. studiare
5. cercare
6. lavorare
7. spiegare

B. RESPONSE DRILL-Answer the following questions with Lei(formale) commands as per example:

Aspetto?   Sì, aspetti, per piacere.
Shall I wait?   Yes, wait please.
1. Ritorno domani?   Sì_____.
2. Mangio adesso?   Sì_____.
3. Continuo diritto?   Sì_____.
4. Cerco il ristorante?   Sì_____.

SECTION X REVIEW QUESTIONS (Not recorded)
1. Dove si trova il gabinetto?
2. Aspetto? (Answer with a command form)
3. Studiano molto gli studenti?
4. Dove lavori?
5. Che cosa cercate?
6. Dove andate?   (to the stadium)
7. Abiti lontano?
8. Che cosa necessita Maria?
9. Aspettate la professoressa?
10. Perché vai alla mensa?

REVIEW QUESTIONS (continued)

11. Parli con la ragazza?
12. Non ho il libro! (Make an appropriate exclamation
                    to this)
13. Torno qui? (Answer with a command form)
14. Mamma mia! (Make an appropriate explanation for
                    saying this exclamation)
15. Dov'è l'ufficio postale?
16. Parlate italiano?
17. Dove vanno stasera?
18. Perché?
19. A che ora arrivano gli studenti?
20. Che cosa mangiate adesso?

SECTION XI LEARNING ACTIVITIES

1. After each of the following "useful exclamations"
write a complete sentence with a different -are verb.
The sentence should explain the exclamation. Use your
imagination!.
EXAMPLE: Darn it! I have to work late.
a. Accidenti!   b. Mannaggia!   c. Mamma Mia!
d. Per Carità! e. Maledizione!

2. Compose a short story of approximately 7-8 lines
about "La Professoressa e la classe d'italiano."

3. Select 5 pictures and explain each one using a
different -are verb and as much vocabulary from this
lesson as possible.

4. Interview two other people. Ask them the following
questions. Record their answers and be prepared to tell
someone else about them.
a. Come ti chiami?   f. Ti piace il lavora?
b. Dove abiti?   g. Mangi molto?
c. Dove si trova?   h. A che ora arrivi a scuola?
d. Che cosa studi?   i. Hai lezione adesso?
e. Lavori? Dove?   j. Your own question.

5. Write a summary of your two interviews.

LEARNING ACTIVITIES (continued)

6. Compose five good questions using five <u>new</u> regular
-<u>are</u> verbs that are not in this lesson. You need a
dictionary for this. Be sure you understand the meaning
of the verbs you select.

UNIT VI

OVERVIEW OF UNIT VI

In this unit we will continue restaurant vocabulary and learn the two other groups of verbs: -ere and -ire. We will also learn several useful expressions with avere and practice the indefinite article.

GRAMMAR POINTS PRESENTED

1. Idiomatic expressions with avere.
2. The singular forms of the indefinite article un, uno, una, un'.
3. The present tense of regular -ere and -ire verbs.
4. The polite command form of -ere and -ire verbs.

SECTION I BASIC SENTENCES

A. IN PIZZERIA - PT 1.	AT THE PIZZERIA - PT 1.
Antonio, Cinzia e Maria vanno in pizzeria.	Antonio, Cinzia and Maria go to a pizzeria.
Hanno fame.	They are hungry.(have hunger)
Maria ha sete.	Maria is thirsty.(has thirst)
Non c'è posto.	There's no room.
Cinzia vede una tavola libera.	Cinzia sees a free table.
Si mettono lì(or là).	They sit(down) there.
B. IN PIZZERIA-PT 2.	AT THE PIZZERIA-PT 2.
La cameriera arriva.	The waitress arrives.
Prendono una pizza alle quattro stagioni*	They order(take)a 4 seasons pizza.
Bevono Birra Peroni.	They drink Peroni Beer.

NOTE: *This is a pizza divided into four equal parts; these parts are mozzarella, prosciutto, tomatoes and mushrooms. It's American equivalent might be a pizza with "everything on it."

SECTION II DIALOGS

IN PIZZERIA-PT 1.	AT THE PIZZERIA-PT 1.
Antonio: Andiamo in pizzeria.	Let's go to the pizzeria.
Cinzia: Sì, dopo un giallo, ho sempre fame.	Yes, after a detective movie I'm always hungry. ('giallo' literally means yellow)
Maria: Io ho sete.	I'm thirsty.
Antonio: Pero, non c'è posto.	But there's no room.
Cinzia: Vedo una tavola libera. Ci mettiamo lì.	I see a free table. Let's sit down there.

IN PIZZERIA-PT 2.	AT THE PIZZERIA-PT 2.
Cameriera: Che cosa vi posso portare?	What can I bring to you?
Antonio: Prendiamo una pizza alle quattro stagioni.	We'll have a four seasons pizza.
Cameriera: E da bere?	And to drink?
Antonio: Birra Peroni per tutti.	Peroni Beer for everyone.

SECTION III QUESTIONS
PART I

1. Dove vanno dopo il cinema?   Vanno in pizzeria.
2. Perché?   Perché hanno fame.
3. Chi ha sete?   Maria ha sete.
4. C'è posto?   Sì, c'è posto.
5. Cinzia vede una tavola?   Sì, vede una tavola libera.
6. Dove si mettono?   Sì, mettono lì.

PART II

1. Che cosa prendono?   Prendono una pizza alle quattro stagioni.
2. E da bere?   Bevono Birra Peroni.

SECTION IV <u>SUPPLEMENT</u>

A. OTHER KINDS OF PIZZA

Prendono una pizza margherita.	They order(take)a pizza margherita(with mozzarella and tomatoes)
Prendono una pizza bianca.	They order a white pizza (just spices and oil)

NOTE: Pizza in Italy is very often different from the typical American pizza. Usually each person has his or her own separate pizza and it is eaten with a knife and fork. Beer is the usual accompaniment for pizza.

B. SUPPER

*Per cena c'è: For supper there's:
    la minestra   soup
    una frittata   an omelet
    il formaggio   cheese

NOTE: <u>Cena</u> is normally a light meal, especially if you ate a <u>good</u> pranzo. Cena is normally eaten after 7:00 at night.

C. EXPRESSIONS WITH AVERE

Ho fame	I'm hungry
Ho sete	I'm thirsty
Ho sonno	I'm sleepy
Ho ragione	I'm right
Ho torto	I'm wrong
Ho freddo	I'm cold
Ho caldo	I'm hot
Ho mal di testa	I have a headache
Ho mal di schiena	I have a backache
*Ho bisogno di...	I need to: (plus an infinitive or noun)
-mangiare	-eat
-andare	-go
Ho voglia di....	I want to:(plus an infinitive)
-prendere una pizza	-order a pizza
-tornare a scuola	-return to school

EXPRESSIONS WITH AVERE (continued)

NOTE: *This is the expression mentioned in Unit V that is normally used in place of the verb necessitare. You will hear it used in many ways: I need to eat, to study, to do something,or I need a book, a favor, etc.

SECTION V INDEFINITE ARTICLE (A or AN)
We have used the indefinite article frequently in all of our units. It has four singular forms in Italian.

1. UN - before a masculine singular noun beginning with a vowel and with any consonant except z or s + consonant.

2. UNO - before a masculine singular noun beginning with a z or s + a consonant.

3. UNA - before a feminine singular noun beginning with a consonant.

4. UN' - before a feminine singular noun beginning with a vowel.

NOTE: Since the indefinite article is an adjective it agrees with its noun in gender, i.e. masculine or feminine.

Study the following examples:

A. REPETITION DRILL

C'è un ragazzo	There's a boy
C'è un libro	There's a book
C'è un amico	There's a friend (masc.)
C'è uno stadio	There's a stadium
C'è uno studente	There's a student
C'è una casa	There's a house
C'è un'amica	There's a friend (fem.)

B. SUBSTITUTION DRILL
Ho un amico.

_____ libro   _____ amica
_____ casa   _____ lezione

C. SUBSTITUTION DRILL
Andiamo al cinema con una ragazza

_____zio	_____studente
_____sorella	_____signora

SECTION VI REGULAR -ERE and -IRE VERBS

In the previous lesson we studied regular -are verbs. There are two other groups of verbs in Italian whose infinitives end in ere and ire. They are also called regular since they,too,follow the same pattern in deriving their forms. Remember too, that we are still in the present tense and everything that applies to -are present tense meanings also applies to -ere and -ire verbs. Again, forming them in the present tense is a simple process. Study the following list of regular -ere and -ire verbs.

prendere	to take	credere	to think/believe
vedere	to see	bere*	to drink
mettere	to put/place	aprire	to open
vendere	to sell	dormire	to sleep
leggere	to read	partire	to leave/depart

NOTE:*Although bere has a different infinitive form and stem, -bev, its endings are regular. Simply learn the stem -bev and go on from there. To find the stem (except bere) of regular -ere and -ire verbs(to which you add the present tense endings) you drop -ere and -ire from the infinitive.

INFINITIVE	STEM
vedere	ved-
leggere	legg-
dormire	dorm-

For the various subjects below you must add the endings indicated in the ending column. The endings for -ere and -ire verbs are the same except for the voi form.

EXAMPLE: PRENDERE

SUBJECT	STEM	ENDING	TYPICAL SENTENCE
io	prend	o	(Io) prendo i soldi
tu	prend	i	(Tu) prendi i soldi
Lei	prend	e	(Lei)prende i soldi

63

PRENDERE (continued)

SUBJECT	STEM	ENDING	TYPICAL SENTENCE
lui	prend	e	(Lui) prende i soldi
lei	prend	e	(Lei) prende i soldi
noi	prend	iamo	(Noi) prendiamo i soldi
voi	prend	ete*	(Voi) prendete i soldi
loro	prend	ono	(Loro) prendono i soldi

EXAMPLE: APRIRE

SUBJECT	STEM	ENDING	TYPICAL SENTENCE
io	apr	o	(Io) apro il libro
tu	apr	i	(Tu) apri il libro
Lei	apr	e	(Lei) apre il libro
lui	apr	e	(Lui) apre il libro
lei	apr	e	(Lei) apre il libro
noi	apr	iamo	(Noi) apriamo il libro
voi	apr	ite*	(Voi) aprite il libro
loro	apr	ono	(Loro) aprono il libro

*Notice that the difference is in the vowel; logically e for -ere verbs and i for -ire verbs. Notice, too, the similarities to some -are verb endings.

A. REPETITION DRILL

Io prendo un gelato	I have (take) an ice cream
Tu prendi un gelato	You have (take) an ice cream

Lei prende un gelato	*Noi prendiamo un gelato
Lui prende un gelato	Voi prendete un gelato
Lei prende un gelato	Loro prendono un gelato
*Notice stress	

B. REPETITION DRILL (Listen and repeat)

Io apro la porta	I open the door.etc:
Tu apri la porta	*Noi apriamo la porta
Lei apre la porta	Voi aprite la porta
Lui apre la porta	Loro aprono la porta
Lei apre la porta	
*Notice stress	

C. REPETITION DRILL (Listen and repeat)

Io bevo una birra   I drink a beer. etc:
Tu bevi una birra   Noi beviamo una birra
Lei beve una birra   Voi bevete una birra
Lui beve una birra   Loro bevono una birra
Lei beve una birra

D. SUBSTITUTION DRILL

Io non dormo bene   Tu_____
Lei_____   Paola_____
Voi_____   I ragazzi_____

E. SUBSTITUTION DRILL

Lui vede una tavola.   Tu_____
Carla_____   Voi_____
Noi_____   Loro_____

F. SUBSTITUTION DRILL

Loro vendono la casa   Lei(formale)_____
Tu_____   Loro_____
Voi_____   Noi_____

G. REPETITION DRILL
(Listen and repeat)

Maria crede nel progresso.
(in progress)
Lei legge molto.
Non dorme bene.

H. QUESTION-ANSWER DRILL
(Answer the following by number)

1. In che crede Maria?
   (nel progresso)
2. Legge molto? (si)
3. Dorme bene? (no)

I. REPETITION DRILL

Le ragazze prendono una
 coca.
Mario e Carlo non bevono
 niente.
Loro partono subito.

J. QUESTION-ANSWER DRILL
(answer by number)

1. Che cosa prendono le
   ragazze? (una coca)
2. Che cosa bevono Mario
   e Carlo? (niente)
3. Partono subito? (si)

K. REPETITION DRILL

Non leggo il libro.
Allora, apro la porta.
Vedo una macchina.

L. QUESTION-ANSWER DRILL
(answer by number)

1. Leggi il libro? (no)
2. Apri la porta? (si)
3. Che cosa vedi? (una macchina)

M. REPETITION DRILL	N. QUESTION-ANSWER DRILL
Prendiamo i biscotti.	1. Prendete i gelati?
	(no, biscotti)
Ci mettiamo qui.	2. Dove vi mettete? (qui)
Beviamo cappuccino.	3. Che cosa bevete?
	(cappuccino)

SECTION VII (Not recorded)

A. Make up questions using -ere verbs. Use as much new vocabulary as possible.

B. Write an original conversation between two people using as many -are, -ere and -ire verbs as possible.

SECTION VIII POLITE COMMAND FORM
    You are familiar with command forms from regular -are verbs. Command forms of -ere and -ire verbs are equally as simple. Simply use the present stem of any -ere or -ire verbs (with the exception of bere which uses -bev) and add an a to it. You now have the polite or formal command form. Remember again that you is not stated; it is understood.

LEI

VERB	STEM	COMMAND FORM	ENGLISH MEANING
prendere	prend	prenda	Take! Have!
dormire	dorm	dorma	Sleep!
bere	bev	beva	Drink!
credere	cred	creda	Think! Believe!

A. Give the Lei(formale) command of the following verbs in Italian.
1. aprire   3. partire   5. dormire 7. vedere
2. prendere 4. bere   6. leggere 8. mettere

B. Response Drill - Answer the following questions with Lei(formale) commands as per example.
EXAMPLE: Apro la porta?   Shall I open the door?
         Sì, apra la porta,   Yes, open the door please.
         per piacere.
1. Leggo il libro? Sì_____   3. Vendo la macchina? Sì___
2. Parto domani? Sì_____   4. Dormo qui? Sì_____

66

SECTION IX REVIEW QUESTIONS (Not recorded)

Che cosa leggi?
Parto domani? (Answer with a command form)
Dove mettono il libro? (lì)
Vendono i gelati nel bar?
Con chi vai al cinema? (zio)
Dove dormono gli studenti?
Prendo il libro? (Answer with command form)
Partite oggi?
Che cosa vede la cameriera?
Apro la porta? (Answer with command form)
Dove andate adesso? (stadio)
Che cosa c'è per cena?
Hai sonno?
Che cosa prendono per cena?
Ti piace il formaggio?
Avete voglia di mangiare?
Dove vanno dopo il cinema?
Che cosa aprite?
Che tipo(kind) di pizza prendono?
Ha ragione la professoressa?
In che crede la studentessa?
Parti in macchina?
Translate into Italian: Let's sit down here.
Hai mal di testa? (No, a backache)
Translate into Italian: She sees a free table.

SECTION X LEARNING ACTIVITIES

1. You are my boss (il padrone/la padrona)
   Give me five polite command forms and then reasons
for them.
EXAMPLE: Close the door please!
         I have to work.

2. Compose an original conversation. Use as many of the
new -ere, -ire verbs as possible.

3. Answer the following questions:
a. Vendono la pizza a McDonald's?
b. Leggi romanzi? (novels)
c. Partite per Roma domani?

67

d. Bevono Coca Cola i ragazzi?
e. Che cosa mettono lì?

4. Match column A with column B.

A.	B.
a. Ho fame	a. bevo Coca Cola
b. Ho sonno	b. studio la lezione
c. Ho sete	c. dormo bene
d. Ho ragione	d. mangio adesso
e. Ho mal di testa	e. ho bisogno della medicina

5. Write a short paragraph about "La Cameriera." You may tell where she works, describe her job, tell how she feels about it, what her patrons order, etc.

UNIT VII

OVERVIEW OF UNIT VII

In this lesson we will learn some other -ire verbs
and continue the vocabulary of places to go. We will
go shopping at various places and learn numbers to 1,000.
We will learn about a certain Italian housewife's shopping
habits.

GRAMMAR POINTS PRESENTED

1. Numbers from 61-1,000.
2. Age - using the verb avere.
3. Other -ire verbs (add isc except in noi and voi
                           forms).
4. The irregular verb stare.

SECTION I BASIC SENTENCES

A. FARE LA SPESA-PT 1.
La signora Rossi fa la
  spesa.
Per primo, va alla
  macelleria.
Poi va all'alimentari.

C'è un supermercato Findus.
Preferisce i piccoli
  negozi.

GOING SHOPPING-PT 1.
Mrs. Rossi is shopping.

First, she goes to the
butchershop.
Then, she goes to the
grocery store.
There is a Findus supermarket.
She prefers the small stores.

B. ALLA MACELLERIA
La signora Rossi non sta
  bene.
Ha sempre male di ossa.
*Compra un mezzo chilo di
  vitello.
*Costa 3.500 lire.

AT THE BUTCHERSHOP
Mrs. Rossi isn't feeling
well.
Her bones still hurt.
She buys a half kilo of
veal.
It costs 3,500 lira.

* A chilo weighs 2.2 lbs.

70

NOTE: * Comprare and costare are regular -are verbs.
You should add them to your vocabulary.

SECTION II NARRATIVE AND DIALOG

A. FARE LA SPESA

GOING SHOPPING

Mia madre fa la spesa quasi *ogni giorno. Certe volte, io vado con lei. Per primo, compra carne alla macelleria, poi va all'alimentari e certe volte alla pasticceria. Mi piace molto la pasticceria. Lei va anche alla farmacia. C'è un supermercato Findus qui vicino pero mia madre preferisce i piccoli negozi.

My mother goes shopping almost every day. Sometimes, I go with her. First, she buys meat at the butchershop, then she goes to the grocery store, and sometimes to the pastry shop. I really like the pastry shop. She also goes to the drugstore (pharmacy). There is a Findus supermarket near here, but my mother prefers the small stores.

NOTE: * It is still quite common for an Italian woman to go out shopping almost every day. Although supermarkets are becoming more and more popular, many women, especially in smaller cities prefer the smaller stores. Also, convenience foods and frozen foods are in no way as popular as they are in the U.S.

B. ALLA MACELLERIA

Signor Bruno: Buon giorno, signora Rossi. Come sta?

Hello, Mrs. Rossi. How are you?

Signora Rossi: (Io) non sto bene. Ho sempre male di ossa.

I'm not well. My bones still hurt.

Signor Bruno: Peccato! Che cosa desidera oggi?

That's s shame. What would you like today?

Signora Rossi: Un mezzo chilo di vitello.

A half kilo of veal.

Signor Bruno: Va bene questo pezzo?

Is this piece okay?

Signora Rossi: Sì, e voglio delle fette fine.

Yes, and I want thin slices.

Signor Bruno: Certamente.

Certainly.

ALLA MACELLERIA (continued)

Signora Rossi: Grazie,   Thank you. How much is it?
  quant'è?
Signor Bruno: 3.500 lire.   3,500 lira.

SECTION III QUESTIONS
A.
1. Che cosa fa la signora Rossi ogni giorno?
2. Carla va con lei?
3. Per primo, dove va?
4. Che cosa compra alla macelleria?
5. Che cosa c'è vicino?
6. La signora Rossi preferisce il supermercato?

B.
1. Dove va la signora Rossi?
2. Come sta?
3. Che cosa desidera oggi?
4. Come desidera le fette di vitello?
5. Quant'è?

SECTION IV SUPPLEMENT
A. THINGS TO BUY AND PLACES TO BUY THEM
1. Compro carne alla   I buy meat at the butchershop.
   macelleria.
2. Compro dolci e paste   I buy sweets and cakes
   alla pasticceria.   (pastry) at the pastry shop.
3. Compro pasta e pane   I buy pasta and bread at
   all'alimentari.   the grocery store.
4. Compro medicina alla   I buy medicine at the
   farmacia.   pharmacy.
5.*Compro sigarette, sale   I buy cigarettes, salt and
   e francobolli alla   stamps at the tobacco shop.
   tabaccheria.
6. Ogni giorno vado al   I go to the market everyday.
   mercato.
NOTE: * It has been the custom for many years in Italy
to buy salt at the "tabaccheria".

B. LANGUAGE

Capisci l'italiano?	Do you understand Italian?
No, non capisco l'italiano.	No, I don't understand Italian.
Capisci l'inglese?	Do you understand English?
il francese?	French?
il tedesco?	German?
il cinese?	Chinese?
il russo?	Russian?
il portoghese?	Portuguese?
lo spagnolo?	Spanish?
No, non capisco l'inglese.	No, I don't understand English.
il francese.	French.
il tedesco.	German.
il cinese.	Chinese.
il russo.	Russian.
il portoghese.	Portuguese.
lo spagnolo.	Spanish.

C. FAMILY MEMBERS

1. Capisce(il)cinese il padre? *	Does the father understand Chinese?
la madre?	the mother
il figlio?	the son
la figlia?	the daughter
il fratello?	the brother
la sorella?	the sister
la nonna?	the grandmother
il nonno?	the grandfather
Si, capisce cinese.	Yes,he/she understands Chinese.

NOTE: *You may omit the definite article if you wish.

2. Capiscono tedesco i genitori?	Do the parents understand German?
i figli?	the children
i nonni?	the grandparents
Si, capiscono tedesco.	Yes, they understand German.

SECTION V NUMBERS FROM 61 - 1,000 (listen-repeat)
A.

61	sessantuno*	100	cento
63	sessantatre	101	centuno*
68	sessanotto*	102	centodue
70	settanta	120	centoventi
71	settantuno*	130	centotrenta
72	settantadue	190	centonovanta
76	settantasei	200	duecento
80	ottanta	295	duecentonovantacinque
81	ottantuno*	300	trecento
85	ottantacinque	400	quattrocento
88	ottantotto*	500	cinquecento
90	novanta	600	seicento
91	novantuno*	700	settecento
97	novantasette	800	ottocento
		900	novecento

1,000 mille   2.000 due mila**

NOTE: * Remember to drop the final vowel before combining with uno or otto.

** The plural of mille is mila.

B. AGE*

Quanti anni hai?	How old are you?
Ho 25 anni.	I'm 25.
35	
67	*The verb avere is used
88	with age in Italian.
93	
103	

SECTION VI OTHER -IRE VERBS

There is another group of -ire verbs in Italian. The only difference between these and those learned in Unit VI is that they add isc before the ending in all persons except noi and voi. Study the following short list of -ire (isc) verbs.

capire	to understand	pulire	to clean
finire	to finish	spedire	to send
preferire	to prefer		

-IRE VERBS (continued)

SUBJECT	STEM	ENDING	CAPIRE
io	capisc	o	I understand
tu	capisc	i	You understand
Lei	capisc	e	You understand
lui	capisc	e	He understands
lei	capisc	e	She understands
noi	cap	iamo	We understand
voi	cap	ite	You understand
loro	capisc	ono	They understand

A. REPETITION DRILL

Io capisco la lezione.	I understand the lesson.
Tu capisci la lezione.	You understand the lesson.
Lei capisce la lezione.	You understand the lesson.
Lui capisce la lezione.	He understands the lesson.
Lei capisce la lezione.	She understands the lesson.
Noi capiamo la lezione.	We understand the lesson.
Voi capite la lezione.	You understand the lesson.
Loro capiscono la lezione.	They understand the lesson.

B. SUBSTITUTION DRILL

Loro spediscono la lettera. (the letter)

Io_____la lettera.   Mia madre_____la lettera.
Tu_____la lettera.   Lei(formale)_____la lettera.
Voi_____la lettera.   Lui_____la lettera.
Noi_____la lettera.

C. SUBSTITUTION DRILL

Io preferisco mangiare.

Lei_____mangiare.   Loro_____mangiare.
Voi_____mangiare.   Gina ed io_____mangiare.
Lo studente___mangiare.

D. REPETITION DRILL

Gina finisce la spesa.
Preferisce tornare a casa.
Pulisce la tavola.

E. QUESTION-ANSWER DRILL

1. Finisce Gina la spesa?
   (sì)
2. Dove preferisce tornare?
   (a casa)
3. Che cosa pulisce?
   (la tavola)

F. REPETITION DRILL
Noi non capiamo il
  francese.
Finiamo la lezione di
  francese.
Preferiamo andare al cinema.

G. QUESTION-ANSWER DRILL
1. Capite il francese? (no)
2. Che cosa finite?
   (la lezione)
3. Dove preferite andare?
   (al cinema)

H. MIXED QUESTION AND ANSWER DRILL
1. Tu pulisci la casa? (no)
2. A che ora finite? (alle 11:00)
3. Spediscono una lettera allo zio? (sì)
4. Dove preferite mangiare? (in pizzeria)
5. Lo studente capisce il cinese? (no)
6. Preferisce studiare o andare al cinema? (andare al
                                               cinema)

SECTION VII THE IRREGULAR VERB STARE (TO BE)
     You have used the forms of the verb stare since
Unit I. Its use has been limited to that of health
with essere being used in all other cases. Study the
following examples.

         Io sto bene.   I am fine (feels fine).
         Gianni sta male.   Gianni's sick (feels bad).

Although stare is said to be an irregular verb, the only
real irregularity is the double n in the loro form. In
all other forms it takes regular -are verb endings in
the present tense.

SUBJECT	STEM	ENDING		STARE
io	st	o	I am	
tu	st	ai	You are	
Lei	st	a	You are	
lui	st	a	He is	
lei	st	a	She is	
noi	st	iamo	We are	
voi	st	ate	You are	
loro	st	anno	They are	

A. REPETITION DRILL
Io sto abbastanza bene.   Lei(formale) sta abbastanza
Tu stai abbastanza bene.   bene.

76

REPETITION DRILL (continued)
Lui sta abbastanza bene.   Voi state abbastanza bene.
Lei sta abbastanza bene.   Loro stanno abbastanza bene.
Noi stiamo abbastanza bene.

B. QUESTION AND ANSWER DRILL
1. Come sta la professoressa? (male)
2. Come stai oggi? (benissimo)
3. Stanno bene i ragazzi? (sì)
4. Come state, signori? (abbastanza bene)

SECTION VIII - REVIEW QUESTIONS (Not recorded)
1. Dove mangiate?
2. Hai cinquanta libri? (no 80)
3. Dove comprate la carne?
4. Preferisci il supermercato o i negozi?
5. Quant'è il prezzo del romanzo?
6. Quanti anni ha la ragazza?
7. Che cosa desidera oggi?
8. Ti piace lo spagnolo?
9. Capite la professoressa?
10. State bene?
11. Puliscono la macchina?
12. Capisci il tedesco?
13. Di che cosa ha bisogno la signora Rossi?
14. Che cosa compra la signora alla tabaccheria?
15. Spedisce la lettera?
16. Compri i francobolli?
17. Quanti (how many) francobolli compri?
18. Finite la lezione?

SECTION IX LEARNING ACTIVITIES

1. Compose an original conversation between a mother and daughter about going shopping.

2. Do the following exercise in Italian: (Write out the answer)
a) $62 + 88 =$ ___   e) $97 + 800 =$ ___
b) $700 + 130 =$ ___   f) $2,000 + 1,000 =$ ___
c) $100 \times 2 =$ ___   g) $120 \times 3 =$ ___
d) $500 - 100 =$ ___   h) $400 \div 20 =$ ___

77

LEARNING ACTIVITIES (continued)

2. (con't)
i) 295 x 3 = ___   j) 325 - 67 = ___

3. Fill in the blanks:
a. Claudia è giovane (teenager), ha ___anni.
b. Carlo è il nonno; ha ___anni.
c. Maria è la madre di Claudia; ha ___anni.
d. Giorgio è il padre di Claudia; ha ___anni.

4. Write out five questions that follow logically to ask someone you know.

UNIT VIII

OVERVIEW OF UNIT VIII

In this unit we will talk on the telephone, learn about the weather, the months and the seasons, the uses of the verb fare, and use possessive forms.

GRAMMAR POINTS PRESENTED

1. Weather expressions with fare.
2. The present tense of the irregular verb fare.
3. Possession with di.
4. Possession with contractions:del, dello, della, dell'.

SECTION I BASIC SENTENCES

A. UNA TELEFONATA
Maria chiama Carla per
  telefono.
Carla non fa niente
  d'interessante.
Hanno una giornata libera.
Fa bel tempo e c'è il
  sole.
Vanno alla spiaggia.
Fanno una passeggiata.

A TELEPHONE CALL
Maria calls Carla on the
  telephone.
Carla isn't doing anything
  interesting.
They have a free day.
It's nice out and sunny.

They go to the beach.
They take(go for)a walk.

SECTION II DIALOGS

A. UNA TELEFONATA
Carla: Pronto!
Maria: Ciao Carla! Cosa
  fai di bello?
Carla: Niente
        d'interessante.
Maria: Allora, facciamo
  qualcosa. Abbiamo una
  giornata libera.

A TELEPHONE CALL
Hello!
Hi Carla! What's up? (What
are you doing)
Nothing interesting.

Then let's do something.
We have a(whole)free day.

81

DIALOGS (continued)

Carla: Sì. Fa molto bello
oggi. C'è il sole ma non
fa troppo caldo.

Yes. It's nice out today.
It's sunny, but it's not
too hot.

Maria: Perfetto per il mare!

Perfect for the ocean!

Carla: Sì. Andiamo alla
spiaggia a Rimini.*

Yes. Let's go to the beach
at Rimini.

Maria: Bene. E stasera
facciamo una bella
passeggiata.

Fine. And tonight we'll
take a nice walk.

NOTE: * Rimini, in north-eastern Italy, is on the Adriatic
Coast and is a celebrated summer resort. It is located
in the Emilia-Romagna region of Italy between the cities
of Ravenna and Ancona.

SECTION III QUESTIONS
1. Chi chiama Carla?
2. Che cosa fa Carla?
3. Allora, che cosa fanno?
4. Perché?
5. Dove vanno?
6. Che cosa fanno stasera?

SECTION IV SUPPLEMENT (Listen and repeat)

A.SEASONS OF THE YEAR

Le stagioni dell'anno sono:

The seasons of the year are:

    la primavera (f.)   Spring
    l'estate (f.)   Summer
    l'autunno (m.)   Fall
    l'inverno (m.)   Winter

B. In che stagione siamo?

What season are we in?

Siamo *in primavera.

We're in Spring.

    in autunno.   in Fall.
    d'estate.   in Summer.
    d'inverno.   in Winter.

NOTE:* The seasons are not capitalized in Italian.
Notice that in for Spring and Fall is in, but d' for
Winter and Summer.

C. MONTHS OF THE YEAR

I mesi dell'anno sono: The months of the year are:

*gennaio	January
febbraio	February
marzo	March
aprile	April
maggio	May
giugno	June
luglio	July
agosto	August
settembre	September
ottobre	October
novembre	November
dicembre	December

NOTE:* The months also are not capitalized.

In che mese siamo?   What month are we in?
Siamo in dicembre.

Che giorno è oggi?   What day is it today?
È lunedì, il
  ventisette luglio.

SECTION V IRREGULAR VERB FARE

Fare, to do or make, is irregular in several of its
forms. However, by now you should have no trouble seeing
the differences and the similarities it has with other
verbs. It's endings are almost those of the present
tense with the exception of the anno form. This is also
true of andare and stare. Study the present tense of
fare.

Io faccio una passeggiata.	I'm taking a walk.
Tu fai una passeggiata.	You're taking a walk.
Lei(formale) fa una passeggiata.	You're taking a walk.
Lui fa una passeggiata.	He's taking a walk.
Lei fa una passeggiata.	She's taking a walk.
Noi facciamo una passeggiata.	We're taking a walk.
Voi fate una passeggiata.	You're taking a walk.
Loro fanno una passeggiata.	They're taking a walk.

83

A. REPETITION DRILL
Io non faccio niente.
Tu non fai niente.
Lei(formale) non fa niente.
Lui non fa niente.

Lei non fa niente.
Noi non facciamo niente.
Voi non fate niente.
Loro non fanno niente.

B. SUBSTITUTION DRILL
Noi facciamo la lezione.
Tu_____.
Voi_____.

Beatrice_____.
Loro_____.

C. SUBSTITUTION DRILL
Stasera (io) faccio una passeggiata.
___tu_____.
___Lei(formale)___.
___loro_____.

___voi_____.
___Carla_____.

D. CUED QUESTION AND ANSWER DRILL
1. C'è il sole oggi? (sì)
2. Gina e Carlo fanno una passeggiata? (no)
3. Cosa fai di bello? (niente d'interessante)
4. Che cosa fate stasera? (una passeggiata)

SECTION VI WEATHER EXPRESSIONS WITH FARE
The verb fare is used idiomatically to indicate weather in Italian. When you say the weather is nice in Italian, you're actually saying it makes nice.

A. REPETITION DRILL
Che tempo fa?	What's the weather like?
Fa bel tempo.	The weather's nice.
Fa molto bello.	It's very nice.
Fa cattivo tempo.	It's bad weather.
Fa caldo.	It's hot.
Fa fresco.	It's cool.
Fa freddo.	It's cold.

There are some other expressions that don't take fare.

B. REPETITION DRILL
C'è il sole.	It's sunny.
C'è un bel sole.	It's nice and sunny.
Piove.	It's raining.

84

REPETITION DRILL (continued)

` Nevica.	It's snowing.
É una brutta giornata.	It's a bad day.
É una bella giornata.	It's a lovely day.

C. CUED QUESTION AND ANSWER DRILL
1. Che tempo fa? (caldo)
2. C'è il sole? (No, piove)
3. É una bella giornata? (No, brutta)

SECTION VII POSSESSION WITH DI
    In English possession is very often indicated with
an 's as in 'she is Paul's wife'. In Italian you can
never do this; 's does not exist in Italian. Possession
is always indicated by the word of in a possessive phrase.
EXAMPLE:

` É la moglie di Paolo.	She is Paul's wife.
	(lit. she is the wife of
di = of in Italian	Paul)

Study the following examples.

A. REPETITION DRILL

É il marito di Gianna.	He is Gianna's husband.
É la moglie di Carlo.	She is Carl's wife.
Sono i figli di Gianna.	They are Gianna's children.
É il fratello di Paolo.	He is Paul's brother.

B. REPETITION DRILL
Il marito di Paola arriva.
I figli di Gianna capiscono l'italiano.
La sorella di Maria crede nel progresso.
Il libro di Gina è qui.

NOTE: In all the examples, the person or thing possessed
or owned precedes di and the person or thing possessing
follows di.

C. TRANSLATION DRILL (Not recorded)
Example: Il fratello di Maria non arriva.
        Maria's brother doesn't arrive.

TRANSLATION DRILL (continued)
1. Johnny's wife isn't talking.
2. Carla's friend (masc.) understands Spanish.
3. Maria's sister studies at home.

SECTION VIII POSSESSION WITH CONTRACTIONS
    Di forms certain contractions when followed by the
definite article. You must know the proper article for
the word so that the proper contraction is formed. Study
the following list of singular articles and their contrac-
tive forms.

il: di + il = del   È il libro del ragazzo.
                              It is the boy's book.

lo: di + lo = dello   Il professore dello
                              studente arriva.
                              The student's teacher
                              arrives.

la: di + la = della   È la figlia della signora.
                              She is the lady's daughter.

l': di + l' = dell'   Cerco il prezzo dell'albergo.
                              I'm looking for the price
                              of the hotel.

A. REPETITION DRILL
È il libro del signore.
Sono gli amici dello studente.
Sono le amiche della ragazza.
È la segretaria dell'avvocato.

B. SUBSTITUTION DRILL
Sono gli amici del ragazzo.
_____signora.   _____madre.
_____zio.   _____fratello.

C. SUBSTITUTION DRILL
È il libro dello studente.
_____università.   _____professore.
_____studentessa.

86

D. CUED QUESTION AND ANSWER DRILL
1. Chi c'è? (il fratello di Mario)
2. Tu parli con la figlia della signora? (sì)
3. È il libro dello studente? (no)
4. Vedete la moglie del professore? (sì)
5. Cercate le sigarette della madre? (sì)

SECTION IX REVIEW QUESTIONS (Not recorded)
1. Cosa fai di bello?
2. Translate into Italian: He's Johnny's friend.
3. Che stagione preferisci?
4. Che tempo fa oggi?
5. Fa freddo in luglio?
6. Hai una giornata libera?
7. Sono gli amici del fratello? (no, sorella)
8. Tu chiami la professoressa?
9. In che stagione siamo?
10. C'è il sole alla spiaggia?
11. Che cosa fate stasera?
12. Carla chiama Maria?
13. È il libro della ragazza? (no, ragazzo)
14. In che mese siamo?

SECTION X LEARNING ACTIVITIES
1. Describe today's weather including the month and the
season in full detail.

2. Using three pictures from magazines, describe situa-
tions and weather based on vocabulary already learned.

3. Make up one question in Italian showing possession
for the following couples:
EXAMPLE: Roslyn and Jimmy Carter.
QUESTION: Chi è la moglie di Jimmy? or
          Chi è il marito di Roslyn?
1. Sophia Loren/Carlo Ponti. 2. Ronald and Nancy Reagan.
3. Paul Newman/Joanne Woodward.

4. Make a telephone call to a friend and plan a day's
activity or outing. Start your conversation with a
greeting and end it properly.

PART 2, UNIT VIII

```
                          UNIT IX

OVERVIEW OF UNIT IX

     In this unit we will expand our knowledge and
vocabulary of adjectives in the singular and continue
possessive forms.  We will also learn some useful travel
vocabulary and the irregular verb volere.

GRAMMAR POINTS PRESENTED

     1. Review of c'è and ci sono.
     2. Plural possessive forms - dei, degli, delle.
     3. The irregular verb volere - present tense.
     4. Volere followed by infinitives.
     5. Singular adjectives and agreement.
     6. The usual position of adjectives.
     7. Common adjectives that precede nouns.

SECTION I BASIC SENTENCES

A. ALL'AEROPORTO              AT THE AIRPORT
Un signore è all'aeroporto.   A gentleman is at the air-
                              port.
C'è un volo per Roma.         There's a flight for Rome.
Parte alle otto.              It leaves at eight.
Vuole un biglietto di         He wants a round trip
 andata e ritorno.            ticket.

B. C'È CARLA?                 IS CARLA THERE?
Mario va alla casa di Carla.  Mario goes to Carla's house.
Carla non c'è.                Carla isn't there.
È alla spiaggia.              She is at the beach.

SECTION II DIALOGS

A. ALL'AEROPORTO              AT THE AIRPORT
Signorina: Buon giorno,       Good day, can I help you?
 posso aiutarla?
```

DIALOGS (continued)

Signore: Sì, c'è un volo per Roma, vero?	Yes, there's a flight for Rome, isn't there?
Signorina: Sì, signore, alle otto.	Yes, sir, at eight.
Signore: È un volo diretto?	Is it a direct flight?
Signorina: Sì, vuole un biglietto?	Yes, do you want a ticket?
Signore: Sì, voglio un biglietto di andata e ritorno.	Yes, I want a round trip ticket.
B. C'È CARLA?	IS CARLA THERE?
Mario: Buon giorno signora Rossi, c'è Carla?	Hello Mrs. Rossi, is Carla home?
Signora Rossi: Ah, Mario! No, Carla non c'è. È alla spiaggia con Maria.	Oh, Mario! No, Carla isn't here. She's at the beach with Maria.

SECTION III <u>QUESTIONS</u>

A. ALL'AEROPORTO
1. Dov'è il signore?
2. C'è un volo per Parigi? (Paris)
3. A che ora?
4. Che cosa vuole il signore?

B. C'È CARLA?
1. Dove va Mario?
2. Con chi parla?
3. C'è Carla?
4. Dov'è Carla?

SECTION IV <u>SUPPLEMENT</u> - GOING TRAVELLING
A.

Vado in aereo.	I'm going by plane.
in treno.	by train.
in barca.	by boat.
B. Necessito un passaporto.	I need a passport.
(Ho bisogno di un passaporto)	
un biglietto.	a ticket.

90

GOING TRAVELLING (continued)

C. Voglio andare a Roma.   I want to go to Rome.
               Milano.   Milan.
               Firenze.   Florence.
               Napoli.   Naples.
               Venezia.   Venice.
               Capri.   Capri.
               Genova.   Genoa.
               Parigi.   Paris.
               Londra.   London.
               Madrid.   Madrid.
               Ginevra.   Geneva.

SECTION V REVIEW OF C'E and CI SONO
        As you already know c'è and ci sono (from essere)
are very useful expressions in Italian. C'è - there is,
and Ci sono - there are, are used in countless ways in
Italian in terms of where objects or people are located.

In the dialog of this lesson Mario says:
     "C'è Carla?"   Is Carla there?
And Mrs. Rossi answers:
     "No, Carla non c'è."   No, Carla isn't (at home).

It is not necessary for her to say,"no Carla isn't at
home", because the expression non c'è means all that.

A. REPETITION DRILL
C'è Mario?   Non, Mario non c'è.
C'è un volo?
Chi c'è?   Ci sono della ragazze nel
                                 bar.

B. CUED QUESTION AND ANSWER DRILL
1. Chi c'è? (Alberto)
2. Ci sono dei ragazzi qui? (si)
3. C'è un volo stasera? (no)

SECTION VI PLURAL POSSESSIVE FORMS
        In Unit VIII you learned singular possessive forms.
There are only three plural possessive forms:
di + i = dei   di + gli = degli   di + le = delle

91

PLURAL POSSESSIVE FORMS (continued)

TYPICAL SENTENCES

Sono i libri dei signori.	They're the men's books.
Cerco la tavola degli studenti.	I'm looking for the students' table.
Sono gli amici delle ragazze.	They are the girls' friends.

A. REPETITION DRILL
È la casa dei ragazzi.
Sono i libri degli studenti.
Sono le macchine delle amiche.

B. SUBSTITUTION DRILL
È l'amico delle ragazze.
_____ signori.
_____ studenti.
_____ fratelli.
_____ signorine.

C. SUBSTITUTION DRILL
Preferisco i libri dei professori.
_____ biblioteche.   _____ negozi.
_____ librerie.

D. MIXED DRILL (all forms singular and plural)
Vedo la tavola del ragazzo.
_____ zia.   _____ signori.
_____ studenti.   _____ nonna.
_____ amico.   _____ genitori.

E. TRANSLATION DRILL (Not recorded)
EXAMPLE: L'amico delle ragazze non c'è.
         The girls' friend isn't in.
1. The students' books are here. _____
2. I prefer the parents' table. _____
3. It's the grandparents' house. _____

SECTION VII IRREGULAR VERB VOLERE (to wish, to want)

Volere is another verb that has several irregular forms. Notice the gl in the I, we and loro forms. Study the following examples.

Io voglio andare a scuola.	I want to go to school, etc.
Tu vuoi andare a scuola.	
Lei (formale) vuole andare a scuola.	

IRREGULAR VERB VOLERE (continued)

Lui vuole andare a scuola.
Lei vuole andare a scuola.
Noi vogliamo andare a
 scuola.
Voi volete andare a scuola.
Loro vogliono andare a scuola.

NOTE: It is very common to see volere followed by an
infinitive. It is a very useful construction in Italian.

EXAMPLE: Voglio mangiare, voglio fare qualcosa, voglio
         leggere un libro.
         I want to eat, I want to do something, I want
         to read a book.

A. REPETITION DRILL (Listen and repeat)
Io voglio un passaporto.   Lei vuole un passaporto.
Tu vuoi   "   "   Noi vogliamo "   "
Lei(formale)vuole "   "   Voi volete   "   "
Lui vuole "   "   Loro vogliono "   "

B. SUBSTITUTION DRILL
Mario vuole mangiare subito.
Loro_____.   Noi_____.
La ragazza_____.   Tu_____.
Io_____.

C. SUBSTITUTION DRILL
Vogliamo guardare la televisione. (to watch t.v.)
Voi_____.   Lei(formale)_____.
Gina_____.   Gli amici_____.
Io_____.

D. CUED QUESTION AND ANSWER DRILL
1. Signore, Lei vuole un biglietto? (sì)
2. Dove vogliono andare? (alla spiaggia)
3. Vuoi parlare italiano. (sì)
4. Volete andare al cinema. (no)
5. Chi vuole guardare la televisione? (Carla)
6. Vogliono prendere un gelato i ragazzi? (sì)

93

SECTION VIII <u>SINGULAR</u> <u>ADJECTIVES</u> <u>AND</u> <u>AGREEMENT</u>

1. We have used many adjectives throughout our units.
As you know, adjectives, just like nouns, are masculine
and feminine. Most adjectives (as most nouns) end in
<u>o</u> or <u>a</u>. Any exceptions to this normally follow the same
rules as those for nouns (Units III and IV) such as
adjectives that end in <u>e</u>.

2. Adjectives in Italian must agree in number (singular
or plural) and gender (masculine or feminine) with the
nouns or pronouns they modify.

STUDY the following examples taken from our units.

> La <u>nuova</u> macchina.
> È <u>bella</u> e <u>nuova</u>.   (referring to the car)
> Che <u>bella</u> ragazza!
> È un vol <u>diretto</u>.
> Il vino è <u>ottimo</u>.

3. Descriptive adjectives in Italian, unlike English
adjectives, normally follow the noun they modify.

4. There are some adjectives that precede the noun,
usually those expressing number and quantity. Also,
the following common adjectives often precede the noun
they modify:

bello - beautiful,handsome   grande - big, large
bravo - fine, good   piccolo - little,small
brutto - ugly   nuovo - new
buono - good   vecchio - old
cattivo - bad(naughty)
These same adjectives may follow the noun, usually for
emphasis or contrast.

5. Adjectives are also used with the verb <u>essere</u> as
predicate adjectives to describe the subject.
> Example: La ragazza è bella.

A. REPETITION DRILL

Il piccolo negozio.
La piccola macchina.
Il nuovo professore.
La nuova professoressa.

B. REPETITION DRILL

Il maestro è occupato.
La maestra è occupata.
Mario è stanco.
Maria è stanca.

C. REPETITION DRILL

La lezione è interessante.
Il libro è interessante.
Il libro è difficile.
La lezione è difficile.

D. SUBSTITUTION DRILL

Il ristorante è grande.
La casa_____.   La tavola_____.
Il libro_____.

E. SUBSTITUTION DRILL

Io sono stanca.

Mario_____.   Mia madre_____.   Il ragazzo_____.

F. SUBSTITUTION DRILL

La moglie è pronta.

Il marito_____.   La cena_____.   Il pranzo_____.

G. CUED QUESTION AND ANSWER DRILL (using anche)
Example: Il libro è difficile, e la lezione?
Answer: Anche la lezione è difficile.

1. Gianni è bello, e Gianna?
2. L'avvocato è pronto, e la segretaria?
3. La macchina è nuova, e la barca?
4. Carlo è libero, e Maria?
5. La casa è grande, e il ristorante?
6. La zia è vecchia, e lo zio?
7. La lezione è difficile, e il libro?

SECTION IX <u>REVIEW QUESTIONS</u> (Not recorded)

1. Signore, dove vuole andare?
2. Sei sposato(a) ?
3. La casa è vecchia, e l'appartamento?
4. C'è Roberto?
5. Translate into Italian - I prefer the girls' table.
6. Vuoi una birra?
7. Com'è il negozio? (piccolo)
8. Posso aiutarla? (make an appropriate response)
9. Il maestro è occupato, e la maestra?
10. Dov'è Carla?
11. La ragazza è cattiva, e il raggazo?
12. C'è un volo per Madrid?
13. A che ora?
14. La casa è grande, e l'aeroporto?
15. Translate into Italian - I need a round trip ticket.
16. Volete fare una passeggiata?
17. Chi c'è?
18. Che cosa vuole?
19. È la casa dei nonni? (No, zio)
20. Com'è la macchina? (use 2 descriptive adjectives)

SECTION X LEARNING ACTIVITIES

1. Describe the following five items with at least two
descriptive adjectives: la televisione, la spiaggia,
il vino, il cinema, il libro.

2. Cut out a picture from a magazine that contains many
items and/or persons. Describe as many items or persons
as you can using descriptive adjectives. You may use
some new nouns and adjectives provided you know their
meaning and spell them correctly.

3. With another person prepare seven sentences about
things, interests or characteristics, that you and the
other person share.
        Example: Mary and I are students at the university.
                 We're intelligent, etc.

PART 2, UNIT IX

1.
A | B | C

2.
A DOMANI | B DOMANI | C OGGI
BIGLIETTO 2527 | PASSAPORTO | PASSAPORTO

3.
A | B | C

4.
A | B | C

5.
A | B | C

UNIT X

OVERVIEW OF UNIT X

This final unit will not contain much new grammatical material. Vocabulary is stressed as is using all that we have learned in the previous units to express ourselves in oral and written Italian.

GRAMMAR POINTS PRESENTED

1. Plural of adjectives (Review Unit III Sec. IX)
2. The partitive construction.

SECTION I BASIC SENTENCES
A. NARRATIVE - ASSISI

ASSISI

Mi chaimo Francesca Palmieri.
Abito ad Assisi. Assisi
si trova in Umbria.* È
una piccola città, pero è
bellissima. Le case sono
antiche e sono di pietra.
Le strade sono strette e
ripide. Ci sono dei fiori
dappertutto. Assisi è la
città di San Francesco e
di Santa Chiara. Adesso
siamo d'estate e molti
turisti sono qui.

My name is Francesca
Palmieri. I live in
Assisi. Assisi is a
little city, but it's
very beautiful. The
houses are old(antique)
and are of stone. The
streets are narrow and
steep. There are flowers
everywhere. Assisi is
the city of St.Francis
and St.Clare. Now we're in
summer and many visitors
are here.

NOTE:* This is a region of Italy located just about in the center. In addition to the lovely city of Assisi, Perugia and Spoleto are found in Umbria.

B. LA CASA E LA FAMIGLIA
   DI FRANCESCA

FRANCESCA'S HOUSE AND
FAMILY

La casa di Francesca non è
grande. Ci sono cinque stanze;

Francesca's house isn't
big. There are 5 rooms;

LA CASA DI FRANCESCA (continued)

la cucina, il salotto, la sala da pranzo, due camere, e un bagno. C'è anche un piccolo balcone. Il marito di Francesca si chiama Roberto. Lavora nel Banco di Roma. È cassiere. Francesca lavora in un negozio per bambini.* Hanno due figlie, Nicoletta e Claudia. Vanno al liceo.

the kitchen, the living room, the dining room, 2 bedrooms and a bath. There's also a little balcony. Francesca's husband's name is Robert. He works at the Banco di Roma. He's a teller. Francesca works in a children's shop. They have two daughters, Nicoletta and Claudia. They go to high school.

NOTE: * It is becoming more and more common for Italian women to work outside of the home, although their main responsibilities are still to the family and the care of the home.

SECTION II QUESTIONS

A. ASSISI
1. Come si chima la signora?
2. Dove abita?
3. Dove si trova Assisi?
4. Com'è Assisi?
5. Come sono le strade?
6. Che cosa c'è dappertutto?
7. In che stagione siamo?
8. Ci sono molti turisti?

B. LA CASA E LA FAMIGLIA DI FRANCESCA
1. È grande la casa di Francesca?
2. Quante stanze ci sono?
3. Com'è il balcone?
4. Come si chiama il marito di Francesca?
5. Dove lavora Roberto?
6. Che posto(position) ha Roberto nella banca?
7. Quante figlie hanno?
8. Come si chiamano?
9. Dove lavora Francesca?
10. Vanno a scuola? (le figlie)

SECTION III SUMMARY (Not recorded)

A. After answering the questions compose your own summary of Assisi. A simple way to do it is to change the verbs to the third person or she form. Do an oral and a written summary.

B. Write the same kind of narrative about your own city.

C. Using the following questions as a guide, write your own story: La Mia Famiglia e La Mia Casa.
   1. È grande la casa?
   2. Quante stanze ci sono? (or l'appartamento)
   3. C'è un balcone?
   4. Sei sposato(a)? (married)
   5. Hai figli?
   6. Dove lavori?

SECTION IV PLURAL OF ADJECTIVES
   The plural of adjectives is formed in the same way as the plural of nouns. Study the following examples taken from our narratives.

Le case sono antiche.   The houses are old.
Molti turisti sono qui.   Many tourists are here.
Le strade sono strette.   The streets are narrow.

A. REPETITION DRILL
Le ragazze sono belle.   I libri sono difficili.
Le strade sono ripide.   Gli amici sono sposati.
Le lezioni sono difficili.

B. SUBSTITUTION DRILL - I fiori sono grandi.
   Le tavole_____.   Le città_____.

C. SUBSTITUTION DRILL (Double item) - In this drill you may have to change both the definite article and the adjective: Le ragazze sono pronte.
   ____paste_____.   ____birre_____.
   ____studenti_____.   ____genitori_____.

100

D. SUBSTITUTION DRILL (Double item)
Preferisco i libri interessanti.
_____ragazze_____ .   _____negozi_____ .
_____lezioni_____ .   _____amici_____ .

E. MIXED SUBSTITUTION DRILL-SINGULAR-AND PLURAL
   (Double item) Pay attention to your verb form.
La casa è piccola.
_____ristorante_____ .   _____città(pl.)_____ .
_____strade_____ .   _____figlie_____ .
_____libro_____ .   _____bambina_____ .

F. CUED QUESTION AND ANSWER DRILL
1. Come sono le ragazze?   (brutte)
2. Come sono le strade?   (strette)
3. Come sono le lezioni?   (interessanti)
4. Come sono le stanze?   (grandi)

SECTION V PARTITIVE CONSTRUCTION
    We have already learned the singular indefinite
article a or an. The plural form isn't always expressed
in English, although it is understood.

Example: I have a book.   I have (some) books.
         He has a friend.   He has (some) friends.

NOTE: This idea of some is called partitive and is always
expressed in Italian. This is not difficult since we
already know the forms and have used them in other units.
They are all the possessive forms both singular and plural.

     Singular: del, dell', dello, della
     Plural: dei, degli, delle

B. REPEITION DRILL - Study the following examples:
Ci sono delle ragazze nel   There are(some)girls at
 bar.   the bar.
Ci sono dei ragazzi nel   There are(some)boys at
 bar.   the bar.
Ci sono degli studenti   There are(some)students
 nel bar.   at the bar.
Ci sono delle studentesse   There are(some)students
 nel bar.   at the bar.

101

REPITITION DRILL

C'è della birra qui.	There's (some) beer here.
C'è del gelato qui.	There's (some) ice cream here.
C'è della pasta qui.	There's (some) pasta here.

C. SUBSTITUTION DRILL (Mixed)
C'è del caffe qui.
_____cappucino qui.   _____frutta qui.
_____panna qui.

D. SUBSTITUTION DRILL
Mangio dei biscotti.
_____paste.   _____spaghetti.
_____dolci.

E. MIXED SUBSTITUTION DRILL-Singular and plural
Prendo della carne.
_____birra.   _____fiori.
_____spaghetti.   _____formaggio.

SECTION VI REVIEW QUESTIONS (Not recorded)
1. Hai una casa grande?
2. Dove si trova Assisi?
3. Abiti in una bella città?
4. Siamo d'estate?
5. Come si chiama la città di San Francesco?
6. Sono strette le strade di Washington, D.C.?
7. Lavori nella banca?
8. Ci sono molti turisti a Parigi?
9. I ragazzi sono cattivi; e le ragazze?
10. Translate into Italian: There's some ice cream
11. Sono nuove le case di Assisi?
12. È piccola UCLA?
13. Dov'è un negozio per bambini?
14. Sei sposato(a)?
15. Vuoi dei dolci?
16. È sposato il Presidente?
17. D'estate, dove vanno i turisti?
18. Ti piacciono i fiori?

SECTION VII LEARNING ACTIVITIES
1. Section III Summary A   2. Section III Summary B

LEARNING ACTIVITIES (continued)

3. Section III Summary C

4. "Una Casa Ideale" - using as much of the vocabulary and structures that we have learned, draw your ideal house or use pictures from magazines to illustrate it.

5. Compose an original conversation between yourself, as Francesca or Roberto, and Nicoletta.

INTRODUCTORY UNIT - ANSWER KEY

Responses for Exercise 6.

1. primo	9. abitano	17. difficoltà
2. cugino	10. Roberto	18. adesso
3. automobile	11. finestra	19. difficile
4. città	12. così	20. vedere
5. perché	13. utile	21. mezzo
6. bello	14. oggi	22. università
7. albergo	15. ottimo	23. America
8. isola	16. studente	24. dove
		25. anno

Response for Exercise 7 Part B.

1. a   2. i   3. u   4. e   5. i   6. d   7. a
8. e   9. o   10. o

Response for Exercise 10 - 'Z' Sounds:

1. voiced   2. unvoiced   3. voiced   4. unvoiced
5. voiced   6. voiced   7. unvoiced   8. unvoiced
9. unvoiced   10. voiced

Response for Exercise 10 Single/Double Consonant Sounds.

1. single   2. double   3. double   4. single
5. double   6. double   7. single   8. single
9. double   10. double

ANSWER KEY TO 'TEST YOURSELF' SECTIONS:

Remember that certain questions may have more than one
correct answer in the dictation.

Unit I - Part I
1. Come ti chiami? - Mi chiamo...
2. È una ragazza? - Si, è una ragazza.
3. Come si chiama il ragazzo? - Il ragazzo si chiama...
4. Dove vai? -(Vado) al cinema.
5. Come stai? - (choice of several answers)bene,male,etc.
6. Che ora è? - Sono le... or È l'una
7. Sta bene la signora? - Si, la signora sta bene.
8. Dove va Mario? - Mario va...
9. Ciao! - ci vediamo, come stai, etc.
10. Come sta Maria? - Maria sta...
11. Sono le undici precise.
12. Non c'è male.
PART II 1.b 2.a 3.b 4.a 5.a
PART III È un ragazzo. Si chiama Carlo. È una ragazza.
Si chiama Maria. Carlo sta bene. Va al cinema. Maria
sta male. Sono le sette.

Unit II PART II
1. Dove va Gianni? - Gianni va...
2. Tu vai al cinema? - No, non vado al cinema.
3. Sali!
4. Carla va adesso? - Si, Carla va adesso.
5. Tredici e trenta - quarantatrè.
6. Che ora è? - Sono le ___ e ___.
7. Chi va al ristorante? Carlo va al ristorante.
8. Tante grazie - (Prego) or di niente
9. Ti piace la lezione - Si, mi piace
10. Non mi piace affatto!
PART II 1.c 2.a 3.c 4.b 5.b
PART III Io vado a lezione. Va anche Gianni. Andiamo
assieme. Sono le otto e venti. Non andiamo al ristorante.
Non mi piace affatto il ristorante.

UNIT III PART I
1. Che giorno è oggi? - Oggi è...
2. Dove andate domani? - Andiamo...
3. Il ragazzo è qui? - I ragazzi sono qui.
4. Chi c'è nel bar? - Maria è nel bar.
5. Chi è stanco? - Gianni è stanco.
6. Sei pronta? - Sì, sono pronta.
7. Come si chiama la moglie? - Si chiama...
8. Ti piace il prezzo? - No, non mi piace il prezzo.
9. Signorina, Lei è studentessa? - Sì, sono studentessa.
10.Com'è la casa? - La casa è nuova e bella.
PART II   1.a   2.c   3.a   4.b   5.c
PART III Oggi è giovedì. La segretaria è occupata. Anche
il commesso è occupato. Domani il commesso è libero e
anche la segretaria. Vanno in macchina e prendono un
caffè assieme.

UNIT IV PART I
1. Sono professori Cinzia ed Antonio? - No,sono studenti.
2. Hai fame? - Sì, ho fame.
3. Dove mangiano? - Mangiano...
4. A che ora andate al giardino? - Andiamo al giardino...
5. L'amico è nel bar? - No, gli amici sono nel bar.
6. L'albergo è qui? - No, gli alberghi sono qui.
7. Ecco gli stadi? - Ecco lo stadio.
8. Ecco i negozi? - Ecco il negozio.
9. Chi è fortunata? - Maria è fortunata.
10.Che cosa prende la studentessa? - Prende...
PART II   ?.a   2.b   3.c   4.c   5.a
PART III Gli studente hanno fame. Vanno alla tavola
calda. Hanno soldi e hanno tempo. Prendono un primo
piatto e un contorno, poi frutta e caffè. Dopo, vanno
alla discoteca.

UNIT V PART I
1. Che cosa spiegate? - Spieghiamo....
2. Parlate italiano? - Sì, parliamo italiano.
3. Dove lavorano i ragazzi? - Lavorano...
4. A che ora arrivi a casa? - Arrivo alle...
5. Andiamo allo stadio
6. Dov'è il gabinetto? (choice of many answers)

UNIT V (continued)
7. Ritorno domani? - Si, ritorni domani.
8. Perché vai alla tavola calda? - Perché (ho soldi) etc.
9. Dove gira il signore? - Gira a sinistra.
10.Che cosa cercate? - Cerchiamo...
PART II   1.c   2.b   3.a   4.b   5.a
PART III   I professori lavorano molto. Non arrivano tardi.
Spiegano le lezioni. Parlano con gli studenti. Tornano a
casa e guardano la televisione.

UNIT VI PART I
1. Partite in macchina? - Si, partiamo in macchina.
2. Che cosa apri? - Apro...
3. Hai mal di testa? - No. Ho mal di...
4. Che cosa vede la cameriera? - La cameriera vede...
5. Ti piace il giallo? - Si, mi piace.
6. Che cosa vendono nel bar? - Vendono...
7. Dove andate adesso? - Andiamo...
8. Ci mettiamo qui.
9. Prenda il formaggio.
10.Avete voglia di mangiare? - No, Abbiamo voglia di...
11. C'e uno studente.
12.Leggi il libero domani? - Si, leggo il libro domani.
PART II   1.c   2.a   3.a   4.b   5.b
PART III   Claudia e Mario vanno a vedere un giallo. Dopo
hanno fame. Allora, vanno in pizzeria. Vedono Gianni e
prendono una tavola libera. La cameriera arriva con una
pizza alle quattro stagioni. Bevono Birra Peroni. Adesso
partono per casa.

UNIT VII PART I
1. Dove comprate la carne? - Compriamo la carne nella
                                    macelleria.
2. Dove si vendono le sigarette? - Si vendono le sigarette
                                         nel bar.
3. Finite il libro? - Si, finiamo il libro.
4. Capisci la professoressa? - Si, capisco la professoressa.
5. Che cosa puliscono? - Puliscono...
6. Quanti libri hai? - Ho.....
7. Che cosa desidera la signora oggi? La signora desidera...
8. Spedisce la lettera.
9. Come state signori? - Stiamo...
10.Ho bisogno dei francobolli (Necessito i francobolli)

UNIT VII PART II
1.c 2.a 3.a 4.b 5.c
PART III Oggi Gina fa la spesa. Per primo, va alla
macelleria. Poi, va al mercato e dopo va alla farmacia
e alla tabaccheria. Compra carne,frutta,medicina e
francobolli. Spedisce una lettera. Finisce la spesa e
torna a casa. Adesso, pulisce la casa!

UNIT VIII PART I
1. C'è il sole oggi? - (choice of many answers)
2. Cosa fai di bello? - Niente, d'interessante.
3. In che mese siamo? - Siamo in...
4. Che tempo fa oggi? - (choice of many weather answers)
5. È il fratello di Gianni
6. Fa freddo in luglio? - No, fa caldo in luglio.
7. Tu chiami l'amico? - Sì, chiamo l'amico.
8. Sono gli zii di Mario? - No, non sono gli zii di Mario.
9. Com'è la spiaggia? - La spiaggia è....
10.Che cosa fate stasera? - Facciamo una passeggiata.
PART II 1.b 2.c 3.b 4.b 5.a
PART III La sorella di Maria crede nel progresso. È
studentessa all'università. Legge molto e quasi ogni
giorno fa una passeggiata. Pero, oggi non fa una
passeggiata. Fa cattivo tempo. Nevica e fa molto freddo.

UNIT IX PART I
1. Sei sposato/sposata? - Sì, sono sposato/a.
2. Chi c'è? - C'è...
3. Com'è la casa? - La casa è___ e ___.
4. Che cosa vuoi? - Voglio...
5. La moglie è vecchia, e il marito? - Anch' il marito
                                        è vecchio.
6. Posso aiutarla? - (many choices)
7. Ho bisogno di un biglietto di andata e ritorno
8. È la casa dei nonni? - No, è la casa...
9. Chi è cattiva? - Nicoletta è cattiva.
10.Preferisce la tavola delle ragazze.
PART II 1.c 2.b 3.c 4.a 5.c
PART III Un signore va a Firenze. Necessita un biglietto.
Parla con la signorina. Vuole andare domani. È fortunato.
C'è un volo diretto domani a mezzogiorno. Il signore
compra un biglietto di andata e ritorno. Poi, torna in
ufficio.

UNIT X PART I
1. Dove si trova N.Y.? - N.Y. si trova...
2. Siamo d'estate? - Siamo...
3. Come si chiama la città di SanFrancesco?
   Si chiama Assisi.
4. È piccola l'università? - Sì, è piccola.
5. Vuoi dei dolci? - Sì, voglio dei dolci.
6. Ci sono dei turisti d'apertutto? - Sì, ci sono dei
                                       turisti d'apertutto.
7. Hai una casa? - Sì, ho una casa.
8. Come sono le strade? - Le strade sono...
9. Dove abiti? - Abito...
10.Lavori nella banca? - Sì, lavoro nella banca.
11.C'e del gelato
12.E'sposata la professoressa? - Sì, è sposata.
PART II   1.b 2.a 3.c 4.a 5.b
PART III   Gino abita in una bella città. È abbastanza
grande. Ci sono delle case antiche e anche moderne.
Gino è avvocato. Lavora in ufficio e poi torna a casa.
Non è sposato. Ha un appartamento piccolo con un balcone.

CPSIA information can be obtained at www.ICGtesting.com
Printed in the USA
270454BV00002B/44/A